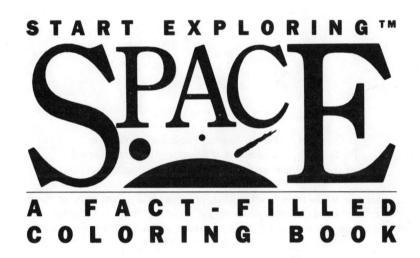

START EXPLORING™
SPACE
A FACT-FILLED COLORING BOOK

Dennis Mammana
Illustrated by Helen I. Driggs

RUNNING PRESS

PHILADELPHIA, PENNSYLVANIA

Canadian representatives: General Publishing Co., Ltd.,
30 Lesmill Road, Don Mills, Ontario M3B 2T6.

International representatives: Worldwide Media Services, Inc.,
30 Montgomery Street, Jersey City, NJ 07302.

9 8 7 6 5 4   3 2

Digit on the right indicates the number of this printing.

ISBN 0-89471-864-9

Editorial Director: Nancy Steele
Editor: Gregory C. Aaron
Cover design: Toby Schmidt
Interior design: Jacqueline Spadaro
Cover, interior, and poster illustrations: Helen I. Driggs
Poster copyright © 1991 Running Press Book Publishers
Typography: CG Century Oldstyle with ITC Franklin Gothic Heavy,
by COMMCOR Communications Corporation, Philadelphia, Pennsylvania

This book may be ordered by mail from the publisher.
Please add $2.50 for postage and handling.
But try your bookstore first!
Running Press Book Publishers
125 South Twenty-second Street
Philadelphia, Pennsylvania 19103.

CONTENTS

INTRODUCTION
The Worlds Beyond

Astronomers are like detectives. They study clues in the sky to learn how the universe works—how it began, and how it may change in the future.

But astronomers can't visit the stars to perform experiments. The nearest stars are too distant, trillions of miles away, and their light takes many years to reach us. Even the planets of our solar system are so far away that humans have never visited them.

So astronomers must use large telescopes, robot spacecraft, and electronic instruments to peer at the light coming from space. They use computers and math to calculate the sizes, temperatures, and speeds of celestial bodies. And they use their minds to *imagine* what a cosmic journey would be like.

That's exactly what we'll do in this book. Ours will be a journey through space and time. We'll begin in your own backyard, and gaze upward at the sights of the night sky. Then we'll leave our Earth behind in search for other worlds. And we'll travel through time—from the days of old to the distant future, to see how stargazers of different ages have worked and thought.

So get ready for an exciting journey of the imagination—a journey through the universe.

Looking into the Night

Late in the afternoon, the brilliant colors of sunset begin to fade. The bright blue sky slowly turns to black, and people gaze upward as the sparkling stars begin to shine.

Many people enjoy watching the stars—teachers, doctors, plumbers, farmers, and students. Stargazing is their hobby. During the day they work hard in school or at their jobs, and at night they take time at home to study the universe. These people are called amateur astronomers.

Amateur astronomers can recognize the beautiful patterns of stars—the constellations. They watch as the moon and planets wander across the stars from month to month. And they view other cosmic events such as shooting stars, comets, and eclipses of the moon and sun.

Some amateurs even build or buy telescopes to get a closer look at the sky. Some draw maps of the moon or planets, watch stars that change their brightness, or search for new comets. And they join clubs of other amateur astronomers to talk about the sky.

Astronomy is a fun hobby. To begin, all you have to do is go outdoors and look up!

On clear nights, the sky is your window on the universe.

Sunset

Late in the afternoon, watch as the sun slowly sets in the west. If it is a clear or partly cloudy day, the sky turns to brilliant, glowing colors. Where do these colors come from? Believe it or not, they come from the sun itself.

Sunlight is white, but a glass prism can break it into a beautiful rainbow of colors—red, orange, yellow, green, blue, and violet. This band of colors is called the *spectrum*. The spectrum is always present in sunlight, but the prism spreads the colors out so we can see them.

During the day, our sky looks blue because the air reflects the sun's blue light. Later in the afternoon, the sun dips lower in the sky, and its light passes through more air. As the sun sets in the west, all of its violet and blue light is taken away by the sky. Most of the colors that are left are red, orange, and yellow.

When this colored light strikes the clouds and dust in our air, it illuminates them with brilliant colors. These colors can also appear at sunrise, but most of us aren't awake to see them.

Not all the activity occurs in direction of the sun. In fact, something fascinating happens on the opposite side of the sky. A few minutes after sunset, turn your back toward the west, where the sun disappeared. If you have a clear sky, you might see a large, purple haze near the horizon in the east. This is the shadow of the Earth.

The Earth's shadow appears again just before dawn. This time, we can see it low in the western sky before the sun rises.

At sunset, the atmosphere filters out violet and blue light, leaving red, orange, and yellow.

Lights at Dusk

Only 240,000 miles away, the moon is our nearest neighbor in space. It circles the Earth about every 27 days. As it moves, the moon seems to change its shape. We call the moon's shape its *phase*.

When we see a round moon in the east at sunset, we call it a *full moon*. When the moon looks like the letter "D," it appears in the south at sunset. This is called a *first quarter moon*.

Once a month or so, just before the sky gets completely dark, we can see the moon in the western sky. At these times, it looks like a banana. This is called the *crescent moon*. It looks like this because sunlight is shining mostly on its far side, and we see only a sliver of its front.

But if you look carefully, you might be able to see a faint outline of the whole moon. Some people call this "the old moon in the new moon's arms." It is caused by sunlight bouncing off the Earth and lighting up the dark lunar surface. This is *Earthshine*.

Every once in a while, the moon moves near a very bright star or planet. But even though this star or planet may appear to be right next to the moon in the sky, it is really millions of miles farther away.

Moonlight is light from the sun reflecting off the moon and onto Earth.

Shooting Stars

Imagine you're looking up at the stars on a clear, dark night. Suddenly, the sky lights up as a brilliant star shoots across the heavens and disappears into the darkness.

What you've just seen is a *meteor*. Some people call this a shooting star or falling star. Meteors aren't stars at all, though. They are tiny specks of dust that fall into the Earth's atmosphere from the vacuum of space. Most meteors are as tiny as a grain of sand.

When a meteor hits the atmosphere, it is traveling very fast—many miles per second. It rubs against the air on its way down, and friction heats the meteor until it glows brightly. Some burst into many colors—yellow, red, green. Some can even leave behind a trail of smoke, or, rarely, one might even explode.

If the night is very clear and dark, you can usually see three or four meteors every hour. But there are times of the year when the Earth passes through swarms of these particles in space, and we are treated to a meteor shower.

SKYWATCH

Here is a list of the best times to watch major meteor showers.

Best Viewing Dates	Shower Name	Best Time to View	Direction to Look	Average Number Each Hour
January 3–5	Quadrantids	4–6 A.M.	north	40–150
April 21–23	Lyrids	3–5 A.M.	south	10–15
May 3–5	Eta Aquarids	3–5 A.M.	southeast	10–40
July 26–30	Delta Aquarids	1–3 A.M.	south	10–35
August 11–13	Perseids	3–5 A.M.	northeast	50–100
October 20–22	Orionids	3–5 A.M.	south	10–70
November 15–17	Leonids	4–6 A.M.	south	5–20
December 13–15	Geminids	1–3 A.M.	south	50–80

Two hundred thousand tons of meteorites fall on the Earth each year. Most meteorites are tiny.

Constellations

On a clear, dark night, thousands of stars shine in the sky. At first, it seems impossible to tell them apart. But after a while, you may notice that the stars form patterns. Some are simple patterns, like squares and triangles. Others are more complex.

Back in the days of old, people used this celestial "picture book" to tell stories. They imagined the stars forming outlines of famous people, objects, and animals. These were called *constellations*

One of the most famous constellations is Ursa Major, the Great Bear. It's difficult to see a bear in the sky, but within it appears something easier to spot. Seven stars form the shape of a bowl with a long, bent handle. This is called the Big Dipper. It shines in the northern sky each clear evening.

You can use the Big Dipper to find other stars and star groupings. If you draw a line between the two stars at the end of the bowl—from the bottom to the top—you will find that they point toward the North Star. The North Star sits above the North Pole of the Earth, and is a handy directional guide at night. If you follow the line backward—from the top of the Big Dipper to the bottom—it points toward Leo, the Lion.

You can also use the Dipper's curved handle to find two bright stars. You can follow the "arc" of the handle toward Arcturus in the constellation Boötes, and speed on toward Spica in the constellation Virgo.

Travelers have always used the Big Dipper to find the North Star.

When Noon Turns to Night

As the moon moves in its orbit around the Earth, it casts a shadow thousands of miles into space. Normally we can't see it, but when the moon passes between us and the sun, its shadow might fall onto the Earth. This creates an *eclipse* of the sun.

If the moon passes in front of only part of the sun's disk, it creates a *partial eclipse*. This usually happens once every couple of years. But if the moon moves directly in front of the sun, the sunlight disappears completely. This is called a *total solar eclipse*. These are rare, and scientists go anywhere in the world to see them.

During a total eclipse of the sun, the sky becomes very dark and the stars appear. Animals think it's nighttime and try to sleep. Then, the sun's outer atmosphere—the silvery *corona*—bursts into view. In only a few minutes, the show is over, and the moon begins to uncover the sun once again.

Solar eclipses would be very frightening if we didn't understand them. People long ago thought that the sun was being eaten by a huge monster. To scare it away, they would go outside and make loud noises. When the sun returned, they would feel as if they had protected the sun from being destroyed. Of course, it always worked!

sKY WATCh

Watching a solar eclipse can be exciting, but it can also be dangerous and can cause blindness. NEVER LOOK AT THE SUN DIRECTLY, even with sunglasses or filters. One safe way to view the sun is to project the image of the sun onto a piece of white cardboard with a small telescope or pair of binoculars. Without looking through the eyepiece, aim the instrument toward the sun and hold up the cardboard about a foot behind the eyepiece. Move the instrument around until the sun's image appears onto the cardboard screen. Focus the image, and you will be able to watch the eclipse safely.

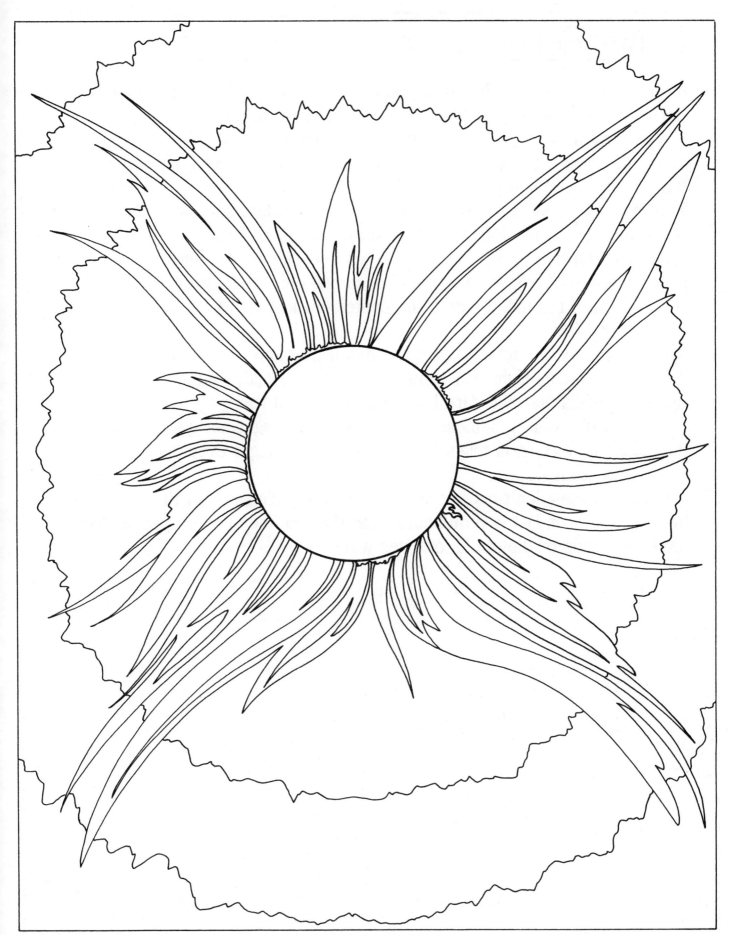

Total solar eclipses reveal the corona around the sun.

Lunar Eclipses

As the moon orbits the Earth, it sometimes passes into the shadow of the Earth. When it does, you might see an eclipse of the moon.

A *lunar eclipse* begins with a bright full moon in the sky. But as the moments pass, the eastern side of the moon seems to get a bit darker. Within only minutes it looks as if a bite has been taken out of the moon. This is the shadow of the Earth. Ancient astronomers knew that its round shape meant that the Earth itself must be round.

During a lunar eclipse, the moon slowly moves into the Earth's shadow. It is called a *partial eclipse* if the moon becomes only partly covered by shadow. But if the moon enters the center of the Earth's shadow we see a *total lunar eclipse*.

At the climax of a total eclipse, the moon may appear a very dark red. This is because sunlight that comes through the Earth's atmosphere turns redder and falls onto the dark lunar surface. But if there are lots of clouds or dust particles in the atmosphere, the sunlight might not get through. If this happens, the moon might become gray, or it might even disappear completely from view.

Lunar eclipses don't happen as often as solar eclipses, but they last longer. Some can last several hours. And they can be seen by people over areas hundreds or thousands of miles wide.

While it is usually possible to observe features on the moon's surface, they are obscured by Earth's shadow during lunar eclipses.

The Aurora Borealis

On some evenings, the sky may light up with beautiful colors. Sometimes these colors appear as waving sheets that come and go, like curtains blowing in a breeze.

These are the Northern Lights, or the *aurora borealis*. People living south of the Earth's equator know them as the Southern Lights, or the *aurora australis*.

People have seen them for thousands of years, but no one understood what they were until recently. These lights are actually caused by violent storms on the sun.

When a storm erupts on the sun, it blasts electrical particles far into space. Some of these come in our direction, and get trapped in the magnetic field of the Earth. As these particles fall inward toward the north and south poles, they make the chemicals in the atmosphere glow in many different colors. For example, nitrogen glows red, while oxygen glows green.

It is difficult to predict when the aurorae will appear because we don't know when a solar storm might erupt. But we do know that people who live in the northern part of the United States and in Canada see them more often than those in the middle or southern parts of the U.S.

When storms rage on the sun, the ghostly aurora borealis appears.

UFOs

People around the world often report seeing strange objects in the sky that they can't identify. These lights are called UFOs.

The letters UFO stand for Unidentified Flying Object. Anything we see in the sky that we can't identify can be called a UFO. But just because we see something we don't understand doesn't mean that it comes from space. Most UFOs are man-made objects such as balloons, dirigibles, hang gliders, or airplanes. Sometimes they can even be oddly shaped clouds, lightning, meteors, stars, or planets.

Some people think that astronomers see lots of UFOs because they are always looking into the sky. But astronomers never see them. That's because they are trained to know what's in the sky and how these objects move. People who see UFOs are usually not familiar with the sky.

Once in a while, UFOs can cause real confusion. During World War II, American pilots followed what they thought was an enemy aircraft. It turned out to be the star Capella. And in the 1950s, Air Force fighter pilots fired their guns at the planet Venus. They missed by several million miles!

UFOs like these flying saucers appear only in the movies.

Early Stargazers

Ages ago, before there were televisions or video games, people sat outdoors at night and watched the stars. As they did, they learned that the sky changed in very predictable ways. The sun always rose in the east and set in the west. So did the moon and stars. The skywatchers of old also discovered that certain stars appeared in the sky only during certain seasons of the year.

Ancient stargazers tried to explain the workings of the cosmos in many creative ways. The Babylonians carefully watched the movement of the moon and planets. They believed that heavenly objects were controlled by the gods, and they tried to understand their motions so that they might predict events here on Earth.

The Egyptians imagined the sky was formed by a goddess named Nut, whose body arched over the land. They believed that the sun, moon, and planets were carried across a celestial river by boats. They used the motions of the sky to develop an accurate calendar, sundials, and water-clocks, and to plan and build temples and pyramids.

The Greeks had gods of the sky, too, but they also believed the universe was controlled by natural processes. They made careful observations and used mathematics to learn clues as to how the cosmos really works. Greek astronomers were the first to suggest that the Earth was a round, rotating planet, that the sun was the center of the solar system, and that the stars were tremendously distant suns.

The Egyptians were among the ancient world's finest astronomers.

Stonehenge

On Salisbury Plain in southern England lies a very large and strange monument. Huge stones sit in a giant circle nearly 100 feet across. In the middle are two horseshoe-shaped patterns of stones. Surrounding the entire structure is a circle of holes filled with chalk, nearly 300 feet across. And sitting nearly 200 feet away is an enormous stone called the Heelstone.

Some of the stones weigh as much as 50 tons. Many are thought to have been brought there from hundreds of miles away. Building Stonehenge wouldn't be too difficult with trucks, but archaeologists believe it was actually built more than 4,500 years ago. Who were the people who built this amazing stone structure, and how did they build it? No one knows.

Many researchers believe the builders of Stonehenge may have used it as a giant astronomical observatory. From the way the stones are placed, scientists have learned that the sun, moon, and some important stars line up with certain stones at significant times of the year. For example, the sun rises directly over the Heelstone on June 21st, the longest day of the year. Stonehenge's builders might have used the series of holes around the stones as counting aids to help predict eclipses. Others think Stonehenge may have been used as a kind of ceremonial temple, where people celebrated religious rituals.

Today Stonehenge sits near a busy roadway, and has become a popular tourist attraction in southern England.

We know little about Stonehenge's builders—but their work can still be seen.

Galileo's New Order

In the year 1609, an Italian scientist saw things no human had ever seen before. In that year, Galileo Galilei learned about a new Dutch optical tube that made distant objects appear closer. So he put lenses inside a lead tube and built his own.

When Galileo aimed his new telescope toward the heavens, he saw thousands of faint stars along the Milky Way. On the moon he saw craters and mountains. He discovered four tiny moons that moved around the giant planet Jupiter. And he found that the planet Venus displayed phases just like the Earth's moon.

At that time, people believed that the Earth was the center of the universe and that all the stars and planets revolved around it. Galileo's discoveries led him to propose that the Earth is a planet revolving around the sun. Galileo showed his observations to Church officials, because it was their job to approve new knowledge. They were not impressed by Galileo's theory, and ordered him to keep quiet. But Galileo knew he was right, and told people anyway. The Church put Galileo on trial and placed him under house arrest for his disobedience.

Today, we know that Galileo was right. His discoveries started a revolution in astronomy, and forever changed the way people think about the universe.

Galileo's simple telescope opened the eyes of the world.

The Mind of Newton

Even as a child in the 17th century, Isaac Newton was a scientific wizard. He spent all his spare time building inventions and thinking about scientific problems.

One day Newton sat beneath an apple tree, deep in thought. Suddenly an apple fell to the ground. Newton concluded that a force must have pulled the apple downward. He also realized that this same force must keep the moon in orbit around the Earth, and the planets in orbit around the sun. Newton became the first person to describe gravity.

Newton was also fascinated with telescopes, but when he built them he was annoyed by the bands of color he saw around the objects he was viewing. To find out where these came from, he took a glass prism and let sunlight shine through it. The light was spread into the rainbow of colors— red, orange, yellow, green, blue, and violet—we call the spectrum.

Newton didn't know how the glass made these colors. But when he put another prism in the colored beam, the colors combined and the beam became white again! Newton discovered that the colors were always there. The glass prism split the white light into colors that he could see.

To correct the problem of white light being split into colors in his telescope lenses, Newton built the first telescope using a mirror. Today, this type of telescope is still called a Newtonian telescope.

GATHERING STARLIGHT

Galileo's telescope was called a refractor, *and was a very simple device. Today's refractors work the same way. A lens catches light from the sky and focuses it into an image. An eyepiece then magnifies this image for the astronomer to see.*

Reflector telescopes, like Newton's, use mirrors instead of lenses. A large mirror catches starlight and sends it back up the telescope tube. A second mirror reflects this light to the side of the tube, where it creates an image. An eyepiece magnifies the image.

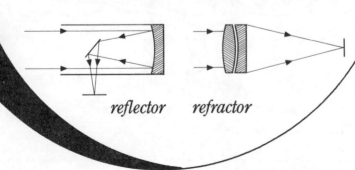

reflector   *refractor*

Newton's discoveries about light, color, and optics made modern astronomy possible.

A Vision of Mars

Over the years, astronomers built larger and larger telescopes. At the end of the 19th century, one of the largest was built in Arizona by a wealthy Boston businessman named Percival Lowell. Astronomy was his hobby.

After visiting many places in the western U.S., Lowell decided that the best site for his observatory was on a hill near the town of Flagstaff. There he built the Lowell Observatory, and the 24-inch telescope inside.

Lowell built this huge instrument to study the planet Mars. To get a good clear view of the Red Planet, Lowell had to stare for long hours through his telescope, waiting for moments of perfect clarity. This was not always easy, especially during the long nights of winter, when cold filled the open dome of the observatory. Only an astronomer who loved his work could have endured such conditions. And then, when the sky would clear for a moment, Lowell would sketch the image of Mars.

What he saw was worth the effort. Night after night he watched as the planet's polar ice caps grew and shrank with the Martian seasons. He watched as the planet's greenish areas of color gave way to brown, and then back again. Most interesting to Lowell were the many fine lines he saw crossing Mars's surface. Lowell believed that these lines were canals built by intelligent Martians to carry water for crops.

Lowell wrote many books and articles about his discoveries, and spoke about them wherever he could. Today we know that the canals he saw were just an optical illusion, but his writings encouraged many children and adults to wonder about Mars as a world to visit, and inspired other astronomers to study it through bigger and better telescopes.

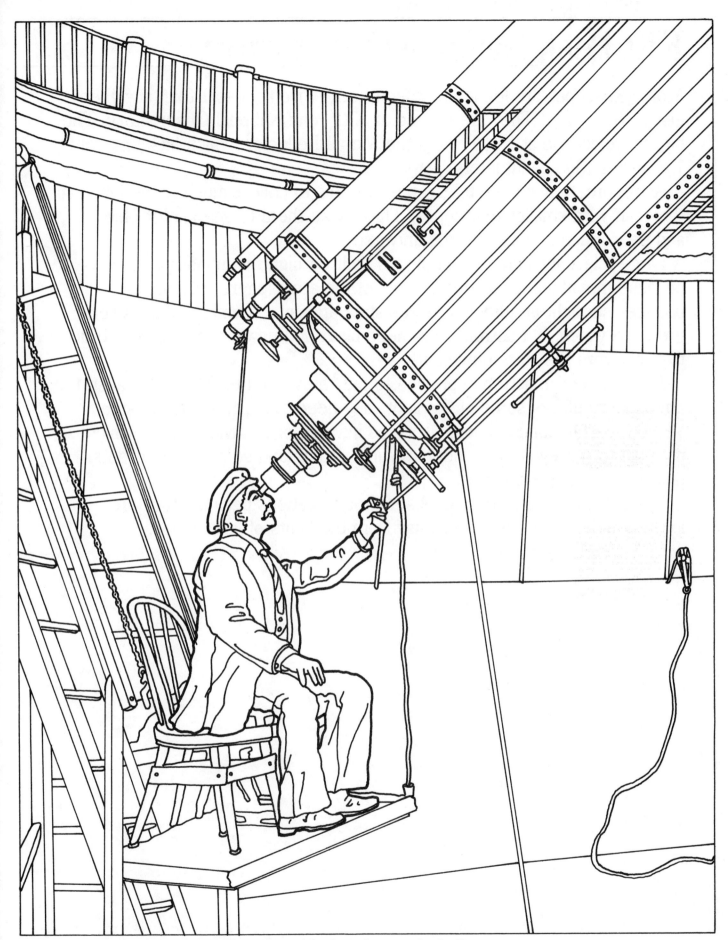

Lowell spent long hours in this room with the telescope he built.

Kitt Peak National Observatory

More telescopes are found in the southern Arizona desert than anywhere else in the world. They are located at Kitt Peak National Observatory. The biggest telescope at Kitt Peak is the Mayall Reflector, which has a mirror 158 inches (395 centimeters) across.

Astronomers use large telescopes like this to collect much more light than they can with smaller telescopes. This allows them to see fainter objects and peer much deeper into the universe.

Large telescopes are almost always built on high mountaintops. This is because mountaintops lie above most of the atmosphere. Moving air bounces starlight around and makes stars appear to twinkle. This is very pretty to watch, but astronomers need clear and unwavering views in order to learn from the stars they see.

Another reason astronomers like to put telescopes up high is because the atmosphere blocks some of the light they need to learn about the stars. Without certain kinds of light—such as infrared or ultraviolet light, which is invisible to our eyes—astronomers can't understand some of the events taking place in the universe.

Mountaintops are also good observatory locations because they are located under dark, clear skies, far from the lights of large cities.

Far from city lights, Kitt Peak attracts astronomers from around the world.

Listening to the Stars

Look around and you can see light of many different colors: red, orange, yellow, green, blue, and violet. These are the colors of visible light, and they form the spectrum of colors.

Light comes to our eyes in the form of electromagnetic waves, only a tiny fraction of an inch long. But the spectrum is much bigger than this. It contains other "colors" such as ultraviolet, X-rays, gamma rays, infrared, and radio waves. We can't see these because our eyes are not sensitive to them. Astronomers who wish to learn about the universe know that these radiations carry important scientific clues. To capture and study them, astronomers have designed specialized equipment.

Some of the most exciting "colors" that astronomers study are radio waves. These waves are many times larger than the waves of visible light. In fact, some are as long as a football field. Radio waves come from all parts of the sky. They are created inside distant galaxies, stars, some planets, and in huge clouds of gas and dust within our own Milky Way. Wherever they originate, radio waves tell us things about the universe that we can't learn from visible light.

To catch radio waves, astronomers need very large antennas, much larger than those on a car or a house. These antennas are called *radio telescopes*. Radio telescopes are made not of glass, but of steel and concrete. They are huge dishes, tens of feet across. The largest, located in a depression in the hills of Puerto Rico, is named Aricebo. It's 1,000 feet (300 meters) across!

Sometimes, astronomers hook many radio telescopes together. This helps them to collect fainter radio signals than any one telescope can catch on its own.

The largest collection of radio telescopes is in New Mexico. Called the Very Large Array, it uses 27 dishes. Each dish can be aimed and used separately. They can also be connected. When they are, they can see as much as if they were a single dish several miles wide, and detect signals from billions of miles away.

Radio telescopes like this can be aimed at any object in the sky.

At the Planetarium

Astronomers can do many kinds of work. Some use large telescopes to study the light from stars and galaxies. Others study radio waves collected by huge radio dishes. Astronomers also send robot probes out to visit the planets, and sometimes even visit space themselves to make observations.

But there is another kind of job that some astronomers have. These astronomers don't view the real sky. These astronomers work in planetariums.

A planetarium is a large domed room with seats. Inside, an astronomer uses a large projector to create an artificial sky on the inside of the dome. With the projector, the planetarium staff can show you amazing things about the universe: how it looks, how it changes, and how astronomers are studying it. They can show you the stars, the moon, the planets, and the constellations as they look from your yard at any time of the year. And you can take imaginary trips across space to visit worlds no human eyes have ever seen.

Most large cities have a planetarium, and some small cities do as well. Many astronomers became interested in the sky by visiting these fantastic places when they were young. You can too!

A planetarium's projectors create shows featuring stars, constellations, comets, and special effects.

Blasting into Space: *Sputnik* and *Explorer*

The space age began dramatically on October 4, 1957.

On that day, the Soviet Union announced to the world that it had successfully launched an artificial satellite into space. The satellite was named *Sputnik 1*, after the Russian word for ''traveling companion.'' Only 23 inches (57 centimeters) across and weighing 184 pounds (84 kilograms), *Sputnik* was a polished metal sphere. It orbited the Earth once every 96 minutes and sent back a simple beeping signal. Sputnik showed the world that space travel was possible.

One month later, the Soviet Union launched another satellite. It was called *Sputnik 2*, but it was very different than the first satellite. *Sputnik 2* carried a live dog named Laika, the world's first space traveler. As Laika hurled through space, instruments sent back information about her health.

People in the United States watched *Sputnik 2* pass overhead and became worried. The U.S. and Soviet Union were racing each other to develop new technology and were doing everything they could to become superior to each other. Launching satellites into space was important, for whoever could do this the best might become the most powerful nation on Earth.

After several failures, the United States managed to launch a satellite into Earth-orbit on February 1, 1958. Its name was *Explorer 1*. It discovered an intense region of radiation surrounding the Earth called the Van Allen Radiation Belts.

The race for space was on.

Sputnik 1's *signal could be heard around the globe.*

The First Astronauts

On April 9, 1959, the world was introduced to the first American astronauts. They were Navy Lieutenant M. Scott Carpenter; Navy Lieutenant Commanders Walter "Wally" Schirra, Jr., and Alan B. Shepard, Jr.; Air Force Captains Donald "Deke" Slayton, Virgil "Gus" Grissom, and L. Gordon Cooper; and Marine Lt. Colonel John H. Glenn, Jr.

They were chosen from more than 500 young men because of their courage, their excellent physical condition, their educations, and their skills at testing new aircraft. They spent the next two years testing the equipment and procedures required for space flight. Some people didn't even think humans could survive in space.

The world received a shock on April 12, 1961, when the space capsule *Vostok 1* carried the first human into outer space. He was a Soviet Air Force pilot named Yuri Gagarin. Gagarin orbited the Earth once, then parachuted back onto Soviet soil.

Only a few weeks later, the first American astronaut rode into space. Alan Shepard flew a space capsule named *Freedom 7.* Shepard didn't orbit the Earth, but he did fly higher and faster than Gagarin had. Then, only 15 minutes after launch, Shepard splashed down into the Atlantic Ocean 300 miles from where he had been launched.

ROCK COLLECTING

During the missions of Apollo 15, 16, and 17, astronauts rode around the lunar surface in lunar roving vehicles (LRV). These electric "moon buggies" allowed the astronauts to explore a total of 55½ miles of the moonscape and collect 2,196 lunar samples, or "moon rocks."

Scientists have learned a great deal about the moon by studying these rocks. For instance, we now know that the moon is at least as old as the Earth. Scientists are studying moon rocks to discover if it is possible to make concrete from lunar soil. If so, it could be used in the construction of a permanent moon base.

Most moon rocks are stored in airtight vaults at the Johnson Space Center in Houston, Texas. Some small rocks have been encased in clear, hard plastic and can be borrowed by certified teachers.

The first U.S. astronauts had "the right stuff"—courage, toughness, and intelligence.

A Giant Leap for Mankind

With the world excited about the first humans riding into space, President John F. Kennedy announced that the United States would land a man on the moon before the end of the 1960s and bring him back safely to the Earth.

On July 20, 1969, *Apollo 11* Commander Neil Armstrong stepped from his lunar landing craft. With more than a billion people watching on television, Armstrong became the first human ever to set foot on another world.

As his boot touched the lunar soil, Armstrong spoke words that will always be remembered: "That's one small step for a man, one giant leap for Mankind."

Soon after, pilot Edwin "Buzz" Aldrin, Jr., joined Armstrong outside the lander. Together, they explored and took photos of the lunar surface. They planted the American flag and saluted it. The astronauts also collected samples of lunar dust and rock for scientists to study back on Earth.

High above the lunar surface, Michael Collins piloted the Lunar Command Module. It was an important job, since this was the ship that would take all the astronauts back to Earth when their mission was completed. During each orbit, Collins passed behind the moon. When he did, he lost all radio contact with the astronauts on the surface, and with the Earth itself. He was alone in the darkness, a quarter of a million miles from home.

GETTING THERE AND BACK

When astronauts arrived in orbit around the moon, their craft split into two parts, the Lunar Command Module (LCM) and the Lunar Excursion Module (LEM). The LCM stayed in lunar orbit and carried one astronaut. The LEM dropped slowly to the moon's surface with two astronauts inside. After the astronauts landed the LEM and completed their mission, the LEM itself split into two parts. The top half left the lunar surface, joined the LCM in orbit so the astronauts could transfer to the LCM, and then dropped back to the moon. The astronauts rode the LCM back to Earth.

When they left the moon for the safety of home, the astronauts left behind a plaque that was signed by President Richard M. Nixon. It says: "Here men from planet Earth first set foot upon the moon—July 1969 A.D.—We came in Peace for all Mankind."

Just after noon on July 24, the Apollo craft parachuted into the Pacific Ocean. The astronauts were

Commander Neil Armstrong took the biggest step in history.

A Giant Leap for Mankind, *continued*

pulled to safety by the crew of the aircraft carrier *U.S.S. Hornet*. Just in case the astronauts brought back any lunar germs, they were sprayed with disinfectant and quarantined for three days. As a welcome back to Earth, the astronauts were given the largest ticker-tape parade New York City has ever seen.

Over the next several years, astronauts returned to the moon for more samples, photographs, and experiments. Only 12 human beings have walked on the moon. They describe it as a gray, desolate place with soil as fine as talcum powder. And overhead, appearing as small as their thumbnails, was the beautiful sphere of the Earth, 240,000 miles (384,000 kilometers) distant.

Astronauts haven't visited the moon since 1972. Today, no nation has space-craft capable of a journey to the moon. Perhaps someday we will return.

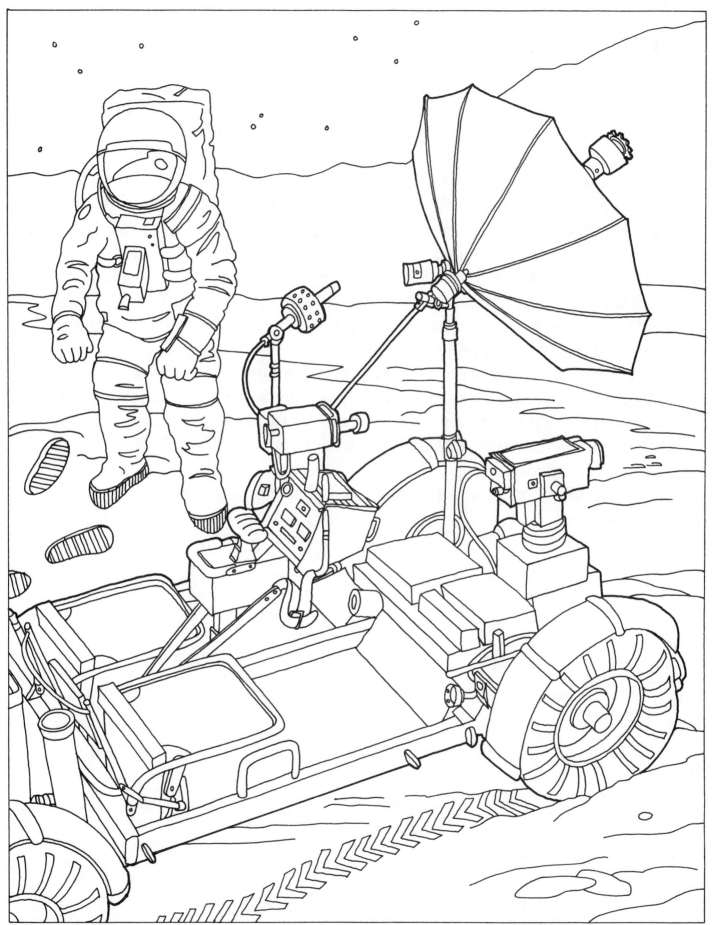

During the later moon missions, electric "moon buggies" gave astronauts the ability to explore miles of the lunar surface.

Apollo-Soyuz

For years, the United States and the Soviet Union competed to be the first into space, the first to the moon, and to beat the other in the "race for space." But the two countries temporarily put aside their differences and planned a joint space mission that took place in 1975.

The Americans launched an Apollo spacecraft into orbit around the Earth, and the Soviets launched a Soyuz craft. As they floated over the world, the spacecraft inched closer and closer together. When they were perfectly positioned, they locked together.

To accomplish this feat, scientists and engineers from both countries spent a great deal of time talking to one another. Each country's scientists had to make sure each understood what the other country's was doing so this mission could proceed safely.

Not only was this mission a success of technology, but it was a mission of friendship as well. In working together, the Americans and the Soviets got to know each other as never before. Once the two spacecraft were docked in Earth orbit, the astronauts and cosmonauts opened the airlock, stepped through, and shook hands.

In one glorious moment, the world smiled at the new friendship that had begun.

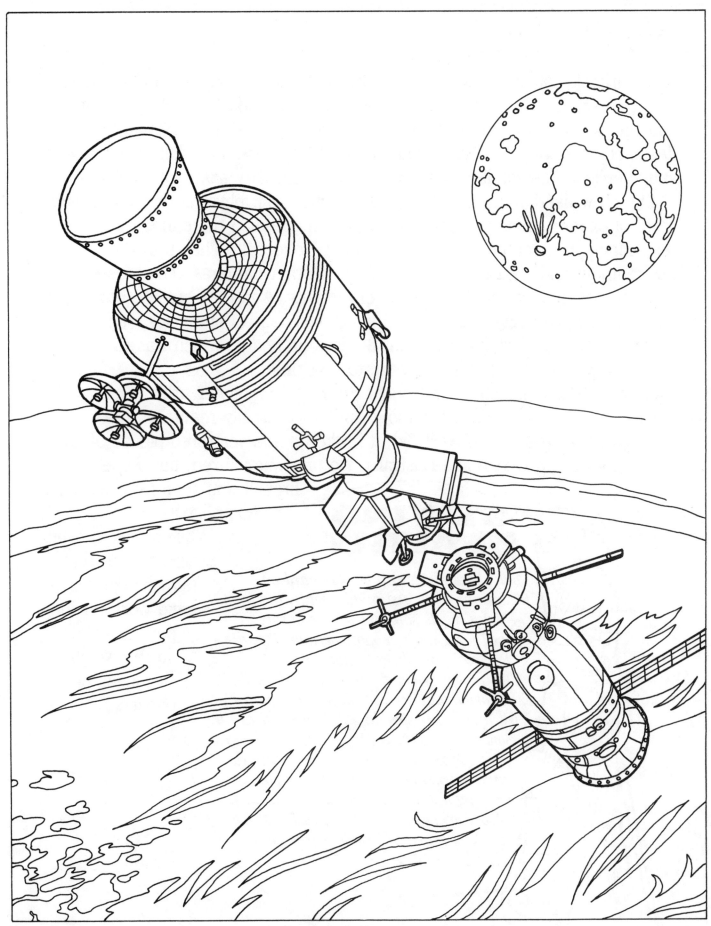

The Apollo-Soyuz docking was a ''handshake'' is space.

Skylab

A remarkable satellite was placed into orbit around the Earth on May 14, 1973.

Skylab was the first American space station. It had a workshop, living quarters for its crew, telescopes, and scientific laboratories. *Skylab* was designed so Apollo spacecraft could fly up to it, dock, and deliver astronauts and supplies. The satellite was powered by electricity from solar cells.

The crew used instruments to perform chemical, physical, biological, and medical experiments. The astronaut/scientists studied the sun with telescopes and took photographs of Comet Kohoutek. They studied the environment and weather of the Earth with other cameras. They tested ways of making new metal alloys in zero-gravity. And they studied how humans react to being in the virtual weightlessness of space for long periods of time. The last *Skylab* crew spent 84 days on board, which was the longest anyone had spent in space up to that time.

After 1974, scientists couldn't boost *Skylab* into a higher orbit. The satellite slowed down more and more until it eventually reentered the atmosphere of the Earth. As it did, it broke up and scattered pieces of itself across the Indian Ocean and Australia. No one was injured, but a spectacular fireball was seen from western Australia.

While it was in orbit, Skylab proved that humans could live and work for long periods of time in the weightlessness of space.

STAYING HEALTHY

Long space flights can be very hard on the human body. Astronauts returning from long flights sometimes have to stay in bed for a week or more because they are too weak and dizzy to stand up.

This is why scientists were amazed in 1988 when cosmonaut Yuri Romanenko reported he "felt fine" after spending 326 days aboard the Soviet space station Mir. This is the longest time anyone has ever spent in space. Romanenko maintained his strength in space by wearing a running suit laced with elastic cords, which resisted his muscles in the place of gravity. He also worked out hard every day.

Skylab *was a flying laboratory and the first U.S. space station.*

The Space Shuttle

During the early days of the space age, rockets were used only once. The United States decided it needed spacecraft that could be used over and over again. This new kind of spacecraft was dubbed the Space Shuttle.

The shuttle is designed to carry cargo to and from orbit, and to help astronauts repair satellites and build space stations. Besides a flight crew, the shuttle often carries mission specialists into space. These are scientists who have special projects or experiments to carry out in orbit.

The shuttles are launched from the Kennedy Space Center in Florida. Each shuttle is 122.2 feet (37.25 meters) long and is 78.06 feet (23.79 meters) from wingtip to wingtip. Three shuttles are currently flying: *Columbia, Discovery,* and *Atlantis.*

Blasting into space, the shuttle acts like a rocket. It is launched from a pad. Attached to the shuttle is a large fuel tank containing liquid hydrogen and oxygen. This fuel is burned in the shuttle's main engines. The shuttle is also boosted by two solid-fuel rockets. Lifted by these powerful rockets, the shuttle goes from the Earth to orbit in just nine minutes. When the fuel tank is empty and the solid rocket boosters are used up, they fall into the ocean, where they are recovered by waiting ships. Coming back home, the shuttle behaves like a glider. Once it reenters the Earth's atmosphere, the pilots land it on a long runway. The shuttle can land either at Edwards Air Force Base in California, or at the Kennedy Space Center in Florida.

HOME AWAY FROM HOME

The absence of gravity makes some everyday activities very complex. For one thing, water does not run down the drain. Instead, it floats in the air in little globes. Stray blobs of water can damage delicate equipment.

Because of this, shuttle astronauts must use a special shower that also works like a vacuum cleaner. Inside this telephone booth-sized cylinder are two hand-held nozzles, one that sprays water and another that sucks it up.

Shuttle meals are prepared before each flight and look like TV dinners. However, astronauts have managed to make sandwiches in zero gravity. The trick is to hold the bread in your mouth while building the sandwich with both hands.

Clouds of steam and smoke billow as a shuttle blasts from its pad.

Onboard the Shuttle

Once in space, the Space Shuttle becomes an orbiting workshop. Aboard it, astronauts can work and play in the weightless environment of space.

Inside the shuttle, astronauts do not have to wear space suits. Instead, they can wear shorts and shirts. The crew compartment has two decks. On the flight deck, a commander, the pilot, and two flight engineers are stationed. On the mid-deck level, there are seats for up to four other engineers and scientists.

The shuttle has carried as many as eight people on a flight. Not all have been American astronauts. Some have been Canadian, Saudi Arabian, Dutch, German, Mexican, and French. Since the shuttle began flying in 1981, only one accident has occurred. The shuttle *Challenger* exploded after launch in 1986. Seven astronauts were killed. The accident was a reminder that space exploration is still a dangerous job.

Once in orbit, astronauts perform a variety of tasks. Some are responsible for keeping the craft in perfect operation. Others do scientific research such as taking photographs of the Earth for meteorologists and geologists, performing research to develop new medicines, and using telescopes to look at special objects. The huge cargo bay is 60 feet (19.3 meters) by 15 feet (4.6 meters) and can hold 65,000 pounds (29,250 kilograms) of equipment or satellites for use in space. It is connected to the living quarters by an airlock.

One of the most exciting shuttle missions was the rescue and repair of the *Solar Max* satellite. *Solar Max* was launched in 1980 to monitor the sun's activity, but it failed after only nine months of operation. In the spring of 1984, shuttle astronauts flew to within a few feet of the satellite, reached out and grabbed it with the shuttle's robot arm, and placed it into the cargo bay. Astronauts went into the cargo bay with their Manned Maneuvering Units (MMUs), repaired the satellite, and sent it back into orbit.

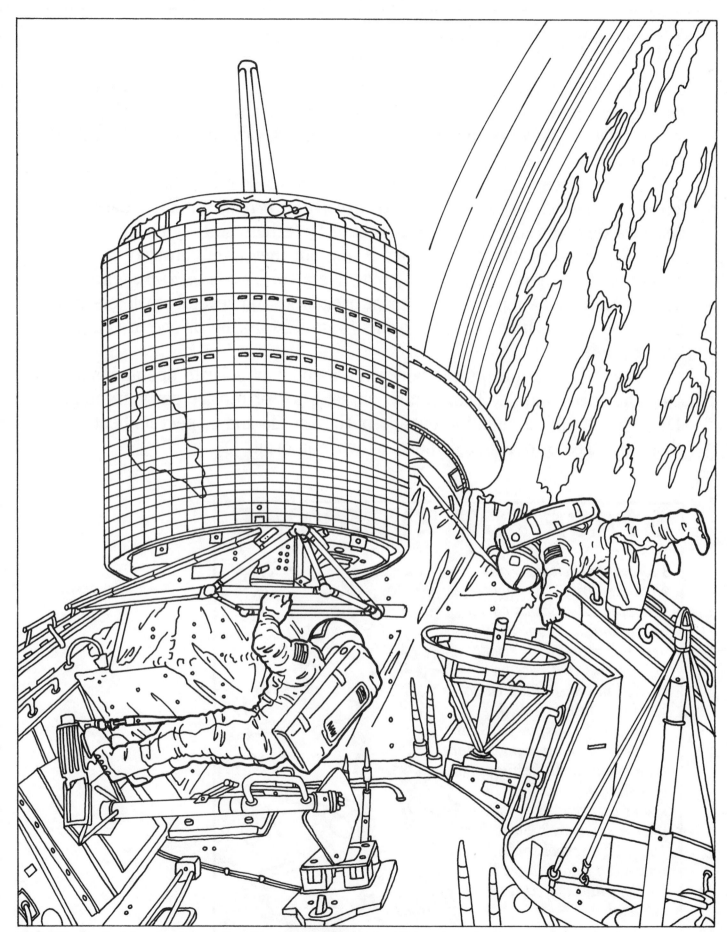

Satellite launching and repair takes place in the shuttle's cargo bay.

Spacewalking

Sometimes astronauts must leave the safety of their craft and venture out into space. They may have to fix equipment or put a satellite into orbit. When they do, they become satellites themselves, orbiting the Earth just as their spacecraft does.

The first space walk was taken in 1965. Soviet cosmonaut Alexei Leonov left his *Voskhod 2* spacecraft for an *extravehicular activity*, or EVA. Early spacewalkers were connected to their craft by tethers so they couldn't float away. Today, astronauts also perform EVAs, but they aren't always connected to tethers. Instead, they may use a *manned maneuvering unit*, or MMU. An MMU straps on like a giant backpack, and several small jets that fire bursts of gas. If an astronaut wants to go forward, he or she fires a jet toward the rear.

With MMUs, astronauts can perform a number of delicate operations far from the space shuttle. They can repair satellites or replace parts in them. They can "walk" around the outside of the shuttle and inspect its heat-absorbing tiles or other equipment, all while in orbit.

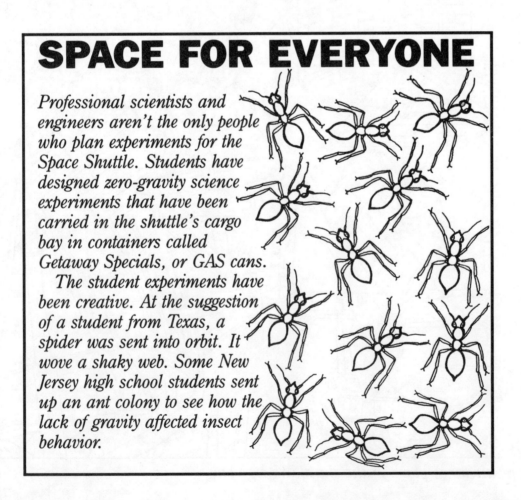

SPACE FOR EVERYONE

Professional scientists and engineers aren't the only people who plan experiments for the Space Shuttle. Students have designed zero-gravity science experiments that have been carried in the shuttle's cargo bay in containers called Getaway Specials, or GAS cans.

The student experiments have been creative. At the suggestion of a student from Texas, a spider was sent into orbit. It wove a shaky web. Some New Jersey high school students sent up an ant colony to see how the lack of gravity affected insect behavior.

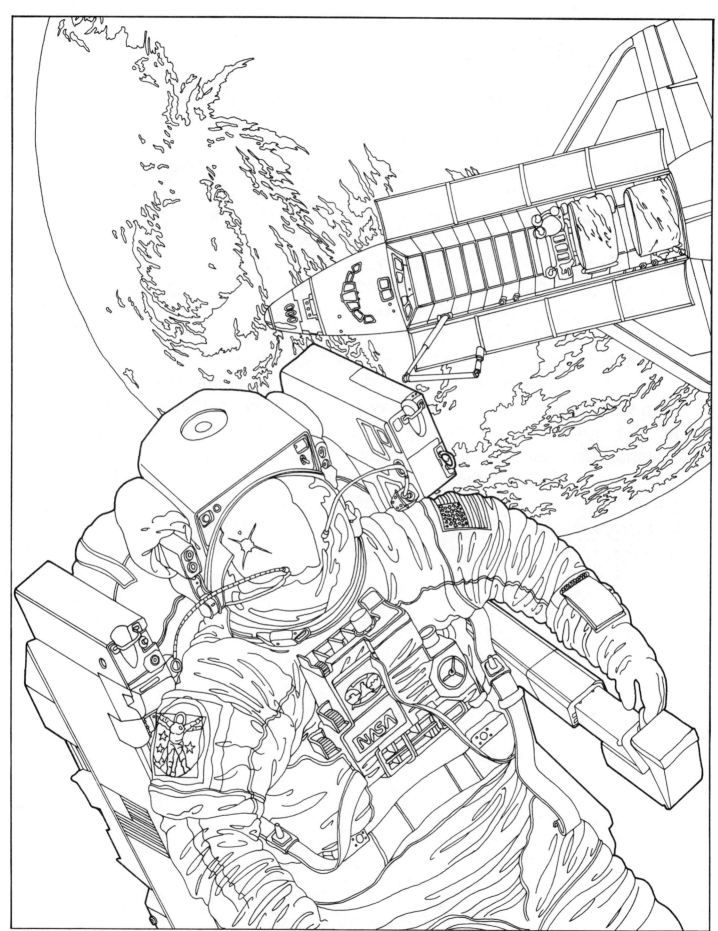

While wearing MMUs, astronauts become human satellites.

Viking on Mars

As exciting as space travel has been, we have only begun the space age. So far, humans have not traveled the great distances to the planets. To do this, scientists and engineers have built robot probes.

Robot probes have sent us photographs and other information from seven planets. One of the most exciting and informative occurred when two spacecraft landed on the red planet Mars. *Viking 1* landed on July 20, 1976, exactly seven years after the first human landed on the moon. Two months later, *Viking 2* set down on the opposite side of the planet. Their cameras showed rolling hills, rocks, boulders, orange soil, and a strange pink sky.

If any life existed here, their cameras didn't show it. So a mechanical shovel dug a small trench in the soil and performed chemical experiments in search of Martian life. Neither lander found signs of life.

Meanwhile, two Viking orbiters circled the planet and photographed it from above. They revealed craters, mountains, extinct volcanoes, and features that look like rivers—but no liquid water! From this evidence, scientists now believe that hundreds of millions of years ago, Mars once had flowing rivers. Some of the water probably escaped the thin atmosphere, but there may be a great deal of water frozen in the soil.

But was there ever life on Mars? No one knows for sure.

The Viking landers found no evidence of life on the barren Martian landscape.

Voyaging to the Outer Planets

Our first close look at the outer planets of our solar system came from two spacecraft named *Voyager 1* and *Voyager 2*. They were launched from Earth in 1977.

The Voyagers encountered Jupiter in 1979 and Saturn two years later. They radioed back photos and other information about the swirling clouds, moons, and rings of these giant worlds.

Then *Voyager 1* headed up and out of the solar system, while its sister craft continued on a different path toward the blue-green worlds Uranus and Neptune. Until *Voyager 2* arrived at Uranus in 1986 and at Neptune in 1989, no one had ever seen these two blue-green worlds up close.

The Voyagers sent their remarkable pictures back as radio signals. They used transmitters that operated with a power of 23 watts. That's only about as powerful as the light bulb in your refrigerator.

After more than a dozen years and a journey of more than 4 billion miles, both Voyagers are still working. They continue to send back information that will help scientists find the edge of our solar system. When they run out of power in the next decade, these spacecraft will continue to drift silently outward toward the stars. They may drift in empty space for a billion years. And just in case intelligent aliens find them, the Voyagers carry messages that tell about Earth, its cultures, and its location in the galaxy.

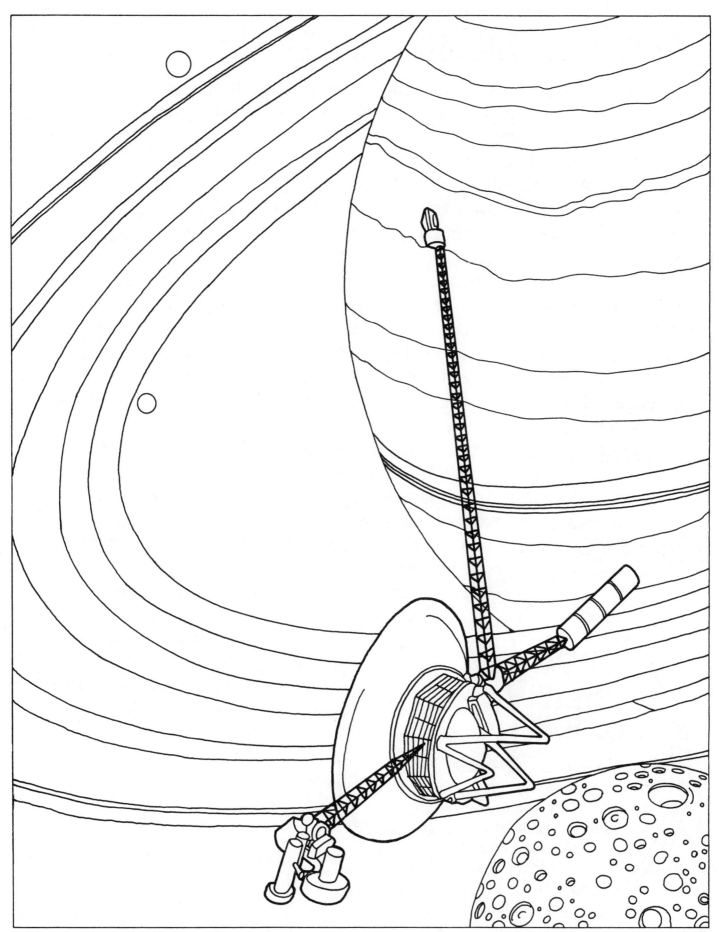

Both Voyager probes flew by Saturn's rings and moons.

Our Star, the Sun

The sun is a star, just like the stars we see at night. It appears big and bright because it is so near. The sun lies "only" 93 million miles (149 million kilometers) away.

If you could go to the sun, you would find that it's a hot, glowing ball of gas nearly a million miles across. The sun has no surface to stand on. Instead, you would find swirling gases with temperatures of nearly 10,000 degrees. Bubbles the size of the state of Pennsylvania rise and sink in the solar atmosphere, and carry heat into space.

From the Earth, astronomers can see huge dark spots on the sun's face. These are called sunspots. They are huge magnetic storms in the atmosphere of the sun hundreds or thousands of miles (kilometers) across. They blast powerful jets of superhot material into space. Astronomers are interested in these strange storms because they interrupt radio communication on Earth. They may even have some effect on the climate of our planet.

The sun emits a tremendous amount of energy. It generates enough power to light 2,600 Earths filled with 200-watt light bulbs. And the sun has been doing this for about 5 billion years.

How does the sun make so much energy? For many years, people thought the sun might be burning like a fire. But today we know that the sun is a giant nuclear furnace. Atoms of hydrogen are rushing around in its center. When they combine they form helium. This emits a tremendous amount of energy. We see that energy as light, and feel it as heat. No life could ever exist on Earth if it weren't for the sun.

HOW MANY IS A MILLION?

A million is a one followed by six zeroes: 1,000,000. If you watched a clock and began counting each second as it passed, it would take you 11 days, 13 hours, 46 minutes, and 40 seconds to count to a million. And a billion is one thousand million!

Solar flares are jets of superhot gas thousands of miles long.

The Swiftest Planet

The nearest planet to the sun is Mercury. Mercury is very small—only 3,032 miles (4,880 kilometers) across. Its gravity is very weak. If you could stand there, you would weigh only ⅓ of what you weigh on Earth. There is no air on Mercury, and the sky appears black even in daylight.

This planet is too small and distant for astronomers to see much detail with even the largest telescopes. In 1974, however, a spacecraft named *Mariner 10* flew by Mercury. It photographed the planet and showed us what Mercury looked like up close.

It found Mercury to be a world of impact craters, cracks, and crevices. It looks very much like Earth's moon. In fact, some people might have wondered if we hadn't sent the spacecraft to the moon by mistake!

Mercury's gray cratered surface looks much like the moon, but its temperature is quite different. Being the closest planet to the sun, its temperature in daylight is 800 degrees Fahrenheit (425 degrees Celsius). In the darkness of night, however, the temperature drops to 200 degrees below zero Fahrenheit (–180 Celsius). No liquid water or life could ever exist on this dry, barren desert.

Mercury is named after the messenger of the Roman gods. It's a good name. The planet Mercury travels 108,000 miles (174,000 kilometers) per hour— faster than any other planet.

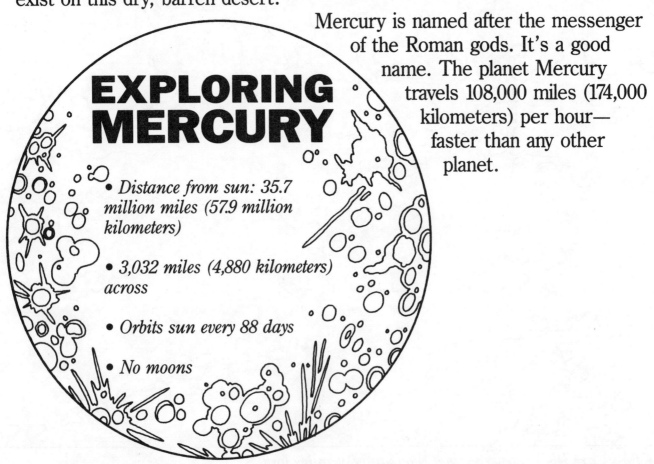

EXPLORING MERCURY

• *Distance from sun: 35.7 million miles (57.9 million kilometers)*

• *3,032 miles (4,880 kilometers) across*

• *Orbits sun every 88 days*

• *No moons*

Mercury's surface is baked, frozen, and battered by meteorites.

Venus

From the Earth, Venus sometimes sparkles brilliantly in the western sky just after sunset, or in the east before dawn. It is a very pretty object to see, and ancient stargazers named it after the Roman goddess of beauty.

Venus looks so beautiful because it is covered with thick clouds. For many years, however, no one could imagine what was going on beneath those clouds. Scientists got some clues from looking with telescopes. But only recently have we learned for sure. The Soviet Union has sent several robot spacecraft into the Venerian atmosphere. The probes sent back reports that Venus is a frightening place.

If you were standing with those probes on the surface of Venus, you would feel temperatures of 900 degrees Fahrenheit (450 degrees Celsius)—hot enough to melt lead. You would be surrounded by an atmosphere of carbon dioxide, and would be sprinkled by rains of acid. Very little sunlight gets through the thick yellow-gray clouds, so the surface around you would be bathed in reddish light.

You might hear low rumbling sounds caused by tremendous lightning bolts blasting on the horizon. And off in the distance you might even see a powerful volcano spewing clouds of dark dust and gas into the air.

In 1990, the U.S. space probe *Magellan* arrived at Venus to map its surface from orbit with a powerful radar. Scientists hope *Magellan* will reveal more about this fascinating world.

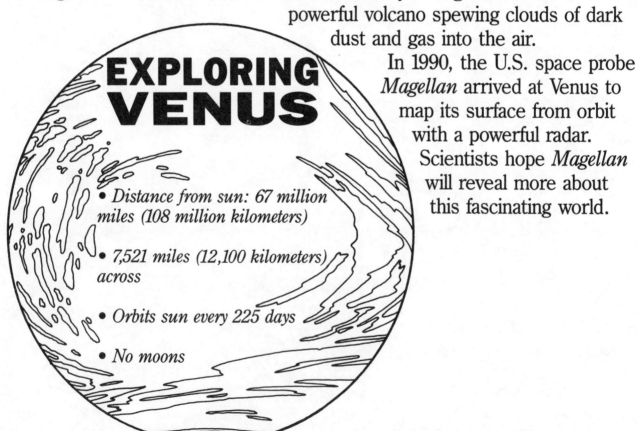

EXPLORING VENUS

- *Distance from sun: 67 million miles (108 million kilometers)*

- *7,521 miles (12,100 kilometers) across*

- *Orbits sun every 225 days*

- *No moons*

Soviet probes like Venera 9 *have sent back photos of Venus's hostile landscape.*

Our Home Planet

The third planet out from the sun is the Earth. We don't often think of our world as a planet. But from space it is an amazing sight.

The first time we really saw the Earth as a planet was in 1968. That year, *Apollo 8* astronauts Frank Borman, James A. Lovell, Jr., and William A. Anders orbited the moon and photographed our world rising above the lunar horizon.

From space we've seen our planet as a magnificent blue and white ball. The water of the oceans sparkles blue. The clouds that streak across its face appear white. And the land appears brown and green.

From space, we can't see boundaries of countries. Religious, cultural, racial, and other boundaries disappear, too. We realize that we all share the Earth as fellow human beings. Right now, 5 billion of us inhabit the Earth.

Only recently have we begun to view our Earth as a vehicle that carries us safely through space. It's the only place we know that has life of any kind. If we damage its ground, water, or air with pollution, we can't get more.

From space we can see how precious our Earth really is.

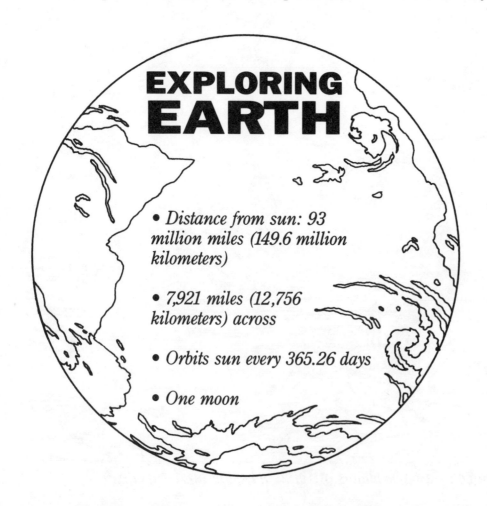

EXPLORING EARTH

- *Distance from sun: 93 million miles (149.6 million kilometers)*

- *7,921 miles (12,756 kilometers) across*

- *Orbits sun every 365.26 days*

- *One moon*

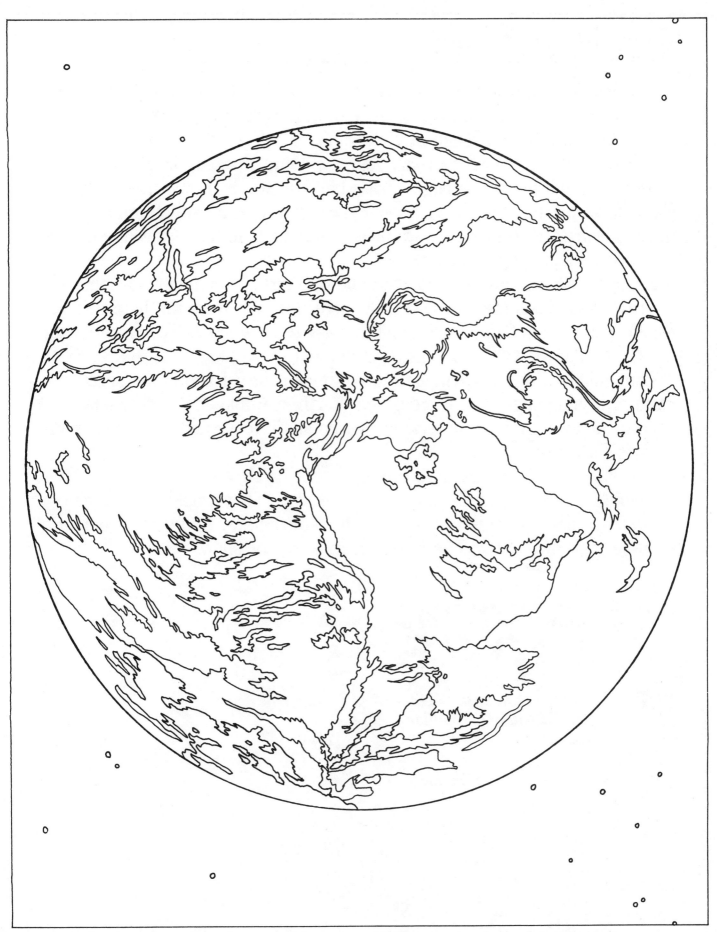

Two-thirds of Earth's surface is covered by water. All life on our planet depends on it.

The Red Planet

For many years, people thought that Mars was a world much like Earth. But recently, we've sent robot spacecraft there for a closer look. We've found that Mars is really very different.

If you could explore Mars, you would see some amazing things. The soil is very red, and the sky is pink. That's because winds of 200 miles (320 kilometers) per hour lift the red soil and carry it into the sky. Sometimes these storms can cover the entire planet with dust. In the sky you would see the sun and two tiny moons.

Explorers would have a wonderful time on Mars. They might visit the canyon called Valles Marineris. It is so large that, if it were on the Earth, it would stretch from San Francisco all the way to New York. By comparison, the Grand Canyon would look like a little ditch!

They might also visit Olympus Mons, the largest volcano in the solar system. It is so huge that, if brought to Earth, it would cover the entire state of Arizona. Geologists (scientists who study rocks and their formation) think it's active.

Martian explorers would have to prepare for harsh weather. The temperature on Mars rarely goes above freezing. They would need oxygen to breathe, since there is very little in the atmosphere. And they would have to bring their own water. The water exists as ice or snow.

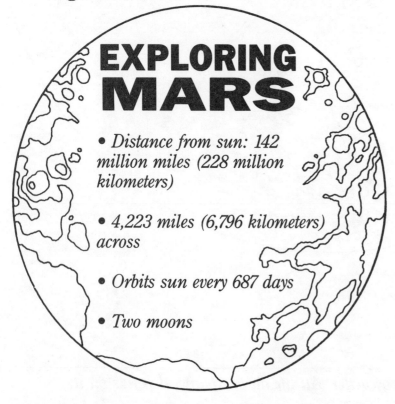

EXPLORING MARS

- *Distance from sun: 142 million miles (228 million kilometers)*

- *4,223 miles (6,796 kilometers) across*

- *Orbits sun every 687 days*

- *Two moons*

From Olympus Mons, lava once flowed onto the Martian plains.

Giant Jupiter

The largest planet in the solar system is Jupiter. Jupiter is so huge that 11 Earths could fit across its face.

We see Jupiter from Earth as a bright star in our sky. If you aim a small telescope in its direction, you can see amazing things. Jupiter appears to have colored stripes running straight across it. If you look carefully, you might even be able to see a large red spot. And next to Jupiter, you might make out four tiny points of light. These are the four moons discovered by Galileo in 1609. They move around the planet from night to night.

Robot spacecraft have shown us these features up close. We've learned in recent years that the colored markings on Jupiter are clouds that swirl in its atmosphere at hundreds of miles per hour. Jupiter is called a *gas giant*, because it is a ball made up mostly of hydrogen and other gases. The Great Red Spot is a monstrous hurricane three times larger than Earth. It has been raging for more than three centuries.

We now know that Jupiter has 16 moons. Some of these moons are made mostly of ice. The most fascinating is the one called Io (EYE-oh). From Io, you would see giant Jupiter hanging in a dark sky. Jupiter's tremendous gravity pulls and stretches this moon, and makes it molten inside. Volcanoes shoot plumes of sulfur into the sky. They cover Io with red and yellow deposits and make it the most colorful world in our solar system.

EXPLORING JUPITER

- *Distance from sun: 484 million miles (778 million kilometers)*

- *88,534 miles (142,796 kilometers) across*

- *Orbits sun every 11.9 years*

- *16 moons*

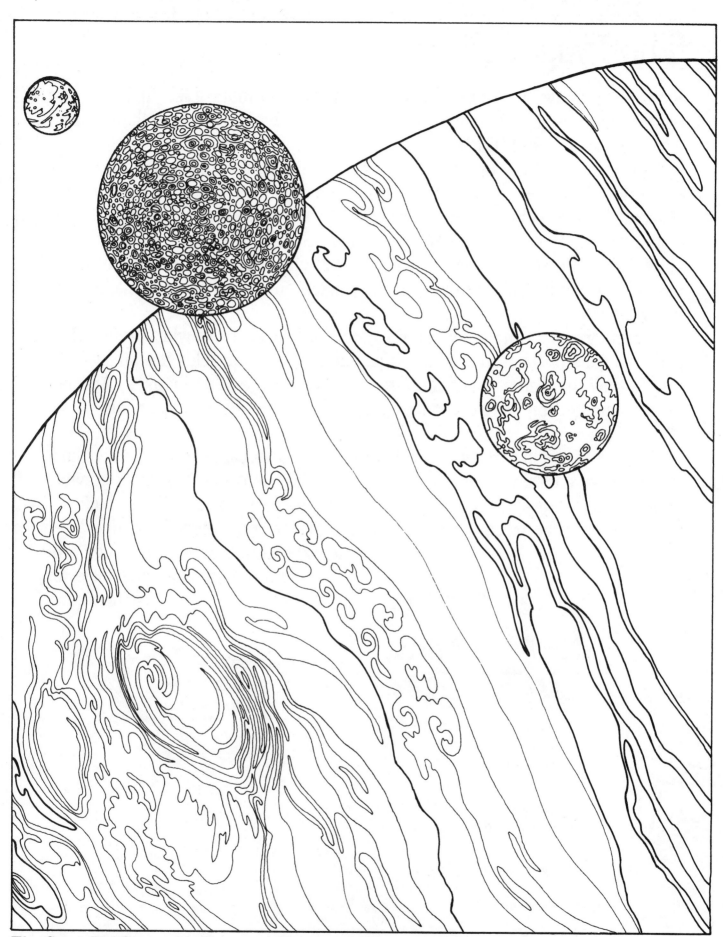

The Great Red Spot, with the moons Europa, Callisto, and Io.

The Ringed Planet

Saturn has always been one of mankind's favorite planets. Like Jupiter, Saturn is a gas giant. Its rings are spectacular. We can even see them with small telescopes from Earth.

The rings of Saturn look solid from a distance. It almost seems like you could ride a bicycle around them. But scientists have learned that this is an illusion. Astronomers sometimes watch Saturn and its rings move in front of distant stars. When this happens, the ball of Saturn blocks out starlight completely. But the rings don't. In fact, starlight actually blinks as the rings pass in front of it. This means that the rings aren't solid, but are made up of many pieces.

Saturn's rings are made of chunks of ice and rock. They whirl around the planet at tens of thousands of miles per hour. Some particles are small— maybe only the size of a pebble. Others may be larger than houses. Anyone or anything getting too close might get hit with one of these tumbling chunks.

Astronomers don't really know where these rings came from. Some think that perhaps another moon once existed around the planet. Saturn's gravity might have torn it apart and scattered its pieces into a disc. Others think that these may be pieces from a moon that never completely formed.

However they formed, the rings provide a breathtaking spectacle for astronomers.

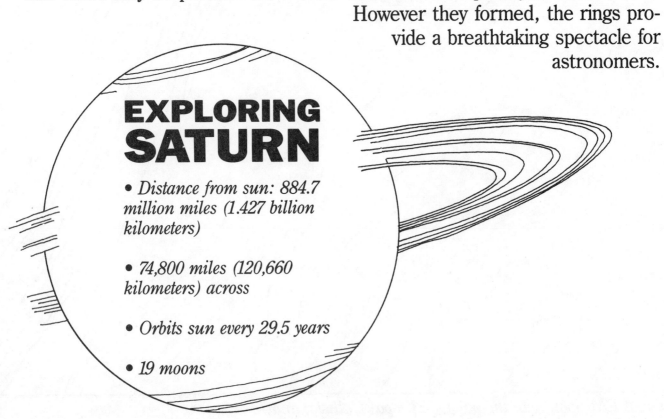

EXPLORING SATURN

- *Distance from sun: 884.7 million miles (1.427 billion kilometers)*

- *74,800 miles (120,660 kilometers) across*

- *Orbits sun every 29.5 years*

- *19 moons*

Saturn's rings are tens of thousands of miles across, but only about 65 feet (20 meters) thick.

Uranus, the Sideways Planet

The first planet ever to be discovered with a telescope was Uranus (YER-uh-nus). William Herschel found Uranus in 1781, as he was searching the stars of the constellation Gemini. Until recently, this planet appeared only as a tiny blue-green dot through even the largest telescopes on Earth.

In 1986, the *Voyager 2* spacecraft whipped by Uranus and radioed back photographs and other information. Today we know that Uranus is a gaseous planet just like Jupiter and Saturn, with no solid surface. But unlike those planets, Uranus doesn't have colorful clouds in its atmosphere. Instead, it looks like a blue-green billiard ball. If this isn't strange enough, Uranus seems to be rotating on its side with its axis sometimes pointing in the direction of the Sun!

Orbiting nearby is a moon named Miranda. Miranda is a bizarre body that has scientists baffled. This strange gray world looks like a jigsaw puzzle that was put together the wrong way. Some people have suggested that Miranda was blown apart ages ago, and that later the pieces came back together.

One of the strangest features of Miranda is a steep cliff. If you could stand on its edge, you could look straight down for 12 miles. And if you tripped over the edge in Miranda's light gravity, it would take 10 minutes to fall to the bottom.

EXPLORING URANUS

- *Average distance from sun: 1.78 billion miles (2.87 billion kilometers)*

- *31,693 miles (51,118 kilometers) across*

- *Orbits sun every 84 years*

- *15 moons*

Uranus looms behind Miranda's shattered surface.

Blue Neptune

Until recently, Neptune had never been seen as more than a tiny blue dot in even the largest telescopes.

Scientists knew that Neptune was a large ball of gas. They knew that Neptune was about 3 billion miles from the Earth, and that it had at least two moons orbiting nearby. Until 1989, that was about all we knew about this mysterious world.

When *Voyager 2* visited Neptune in 1989, scientists were shocked. Neptune didn't look anything like they had expected. It had beautiful blue and white clouds in its atmosphere. They saw great swirling storms—one is as large as the planet Mars, and is now called the Great Dark Spot. Some of the clouds were made of methane gas and were very thin, and scientists calculated that they were more than 35 miles high.

Voyager 2 also radioed back photos of Neptune's moons. Six new moons were discovered. Excellent pictures were taken of Triton, Neptune's largest moon. Triton is a world of nitrogen and methane ice. Temperatures there are near 400 degrees below zero.

As the spacecraft flew by Triton at nearly 61,000 miles (97,600 kilometers) per hour, it photographed two geysers that spewed nitrogen gases into space. The photographs also showed surface features that no one had ever seen before.

Triton's skin is fractured in places, and has dark spots ringed by white bands. There are also ridges that look like the veins on a cantaloupe.

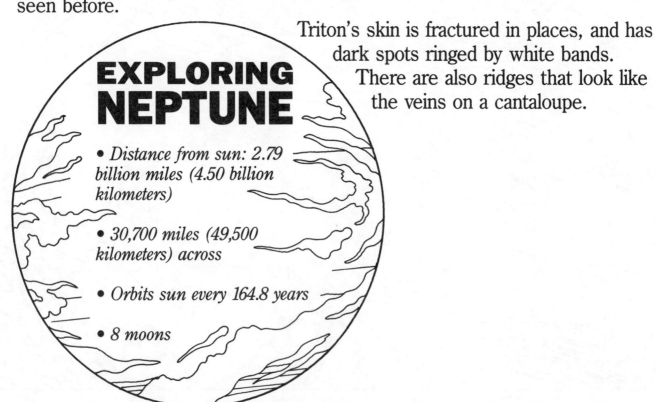

EXPLORING NEPTUNE

- *Distance from sun: 2.79 billion miles (4.50 billion kilometers)*

- *30,700 miles (49,500 kilometers) across*

- *Orbits sun every 164.8 years*

- *8 moons*

Neptune was named after the Roman god of the sea. Voyager 2 recently discovered that the planet Neptune has beautiful ocean-blue clouds.

Mysterious Pluto

The only planet never visited by robot spacecraft from Earth is Pluto.

Percival Lowell knew that some object was pulling on Neptune with its gravity, and he mathematically predicted the existence of an unknown planet around the turn of the century. It wasn't until 1930, however, that it was found. In that year, Clyde Tombaugh sighted Pluto from the Lowell Observatory in Arizona.

To astronomers on Earth, Pluto looks like a faint dot of light. It orbits the sun in a great ellipse that crosses the path of Neptune about every 250 years. Right now, Pluto is actually closer to the sun than Neptune. That will change in 1999, when Pluto crosses back again.

Some people think that Pluto didn't start out its life as a planet, but that it was once a moon that was torn from Neptune. Many questions remain about this mysterious world.

Pluto's icy surface is the loneliest place in the solar system. The Earth and all human beings are 3 billion miles away. On Pluto, you could look into the starry sky, but you couldn't find Earth from that distance. Pluto lies so far from home that even the mighty sun would appear as just another bright star. And the temperature would be so cold that a person would freeze into a block of ice in just a few seconds.

EXPLORING PLUTO

- *Average distance from sun: 3.67 billion miles (5.90 billion kilometers)*

- *About 2,000 miles (3,000 kilometers) across*

- *Orbits the sun every 247.7 years*

- *One moon*

Pluto's moon Charon is about one-third as large as Pluto itself. Some astronomers like to think of Pluto and Charon as a pair of small planets.

The Comets

In the cold, dark depths of space, far beyond the orbit of Pluto, billions of chunks of ice orbit the sun. These are the comets.

Once in a while, one of these pieces of ice is tugged by the gravity of the sun or the giant planets. As it travels inward, toward the sun, the ice begins to vaporize. A cloud of gas and dust forms around it. Then, as the comet approaches the heat of the sun, its gas and dust is blown outward by the solar wind. This forms a beautiful tail that stretches for millions of miles across space. Then, as the comet moves away from the sun, its tail shrinks. And the comet again becomes just another chunk of ice billions of miles away. Some comets return every few years, and some take centuries to orbit the sun just once.

When comets pass near the Earth, we can see them in the sky. Some look quite spectacular. Today we know what they are, but the ancient stargazers didn't. They thought they might be omens. Whenever a comet appeared, people feared that sickness and death would follow, or that a momentous event would take place on Earth. Today, scientists think comets are left over from the birth of the solar system nearly 5 billion years ago.

Comets rotate just like planets do. Jets of dust and gas explode from blowholes in their icy surfaces. Astronomers want to learn more about comets because they may be the oldest objects in our solar system.

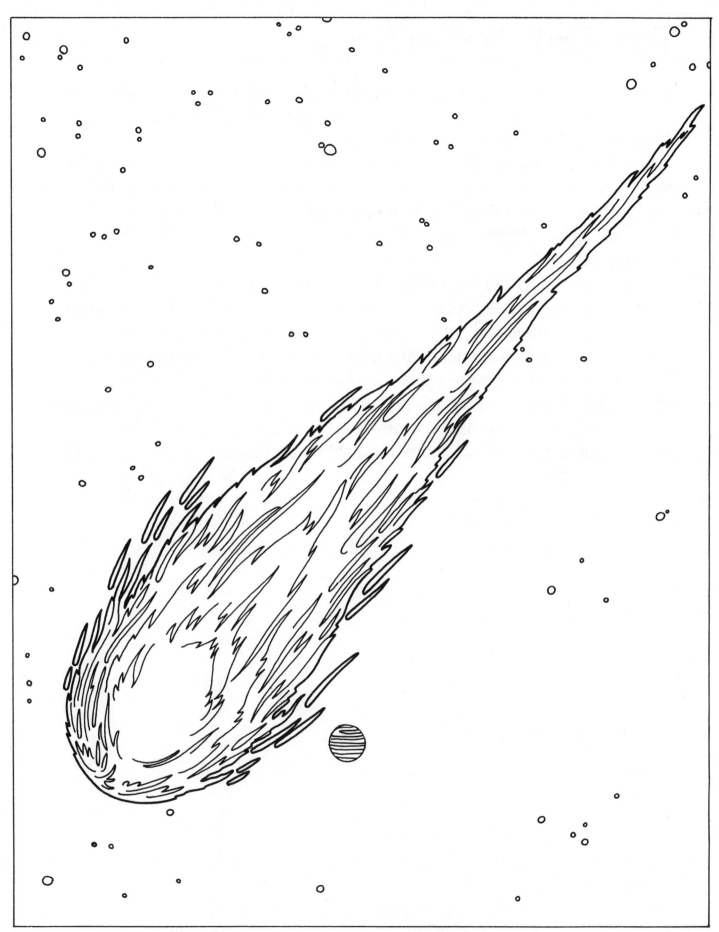

New comets are discovered each year, and old comets sometimes fail to return.

The Birthplace of Stars

Everywhere astronomers look in space they see clouds—not the kinds of clouds we see in our sky, but clouds of gas and dust. These interstellar clouds are called *nebulae* (NEB-you-LAY).

Most nebulae are made of hydrogen, and are very thin. If astronauts were ever to pass through one, they might not even know it. Some interstellar clouds, though, are so thick that we can't see through them. In fact, they look black to us. Other nebulae are lit up by stars on the inside. These we see very easily.

Perhaps the most famous of all nebulae is the Great Orion Nebula. You can see it without a telescope on clear winter nights. It lies just beneath the three "belt" stars in the constellation Orion, 1,500 light years away.

Photographs of this nebula reveal it as a wispy red and white cloud. Astronomers have discovered that the Orion Nebula is a giant stellar nursery. Deep within the cloud, new stars are being born. The gas and dust is collapsing and getting hot, and new stars are igniting all the time. It's these brilliant, newborn stars that are lighting up this nebula from the inside.

Some dust clouds are nurseries in which new stars flare to life.

The Beginning of a Solar System

Stars are born from huge clouds of gas and dust in space. As a cloud collapses under its own weight, it spins faster and faster, and begins to form a disk. At the center, the temperature rises to many millions of degrees. It becomes hot enough for hydrogen atoms to form helium atoms in a tremendous burst of energy. This is how a star is born.

In the outer regions of the disk, clumps of dust and gas form. They grow larger and larger as they orbit the newborn star. These are planets forming from the leftover material of the star's birth.

When the star begins to shine, its energy eventually blows away all the nearby gas and dust. Temperatures are so high near the star that only small rocky worlds can exist. This is how we think Mercury, Venus, Earth, and Mars came to be.

Far away, however, the planets continue to attract gas. The atmospheres of giant planets form. This is how Jupiter, Saturn, Uranus and Neptune were born. Where Pluto came from is still a mystery.

Planets may exist around nearly every star in space. We just haven't spotted any yet.

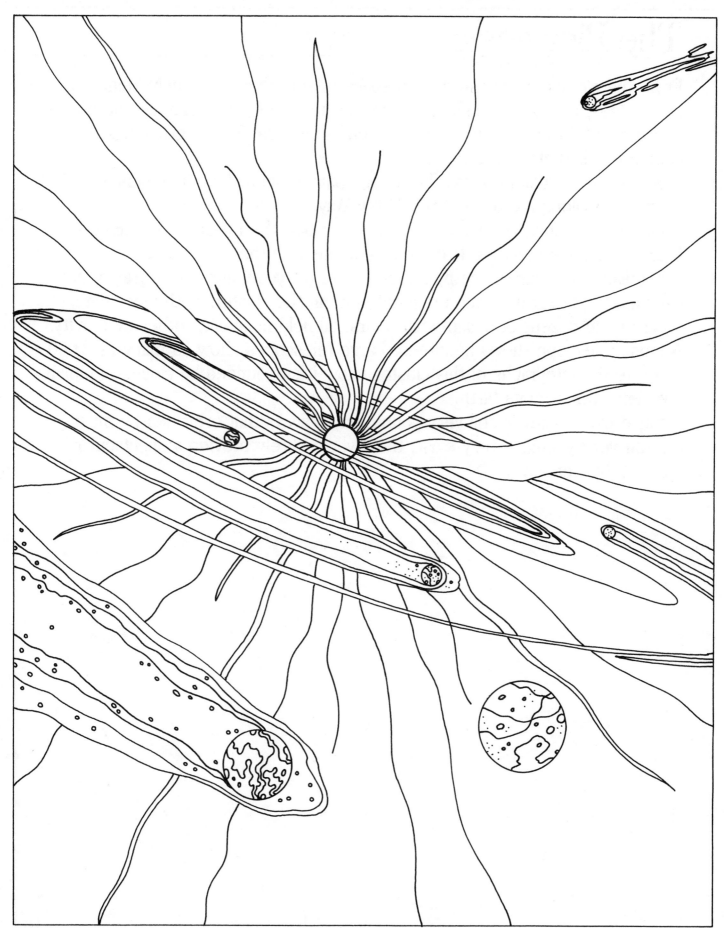

Planets and comets begin as spinning balls of dust and rock.

The Pleiades

From the clouds of gas and dust in space, stars are continuously being born. Sometimes, two or three stars are formed together. Stars can also be born in groups of dozens or hundreds or even thousands. These groupings of stars are called star clusters.

Several star clusters are visible with a pair of binoculars. The clusters all seem to lie along the band of the Milky Way.

One of the most famous star clusters is called the Pleiades (PLEE-uh-DEEZ), or Seven Sisters. It can easily be seen in the wintertime constellation of Taurus, the bull. It lies 410 light years away from Earth. You can easily spot six or seven brightest stars in the cluster. With binoculars, you can see dozens of bluish-white stars, all held near each other by gravity. A small telescope shows hundreds. Large telescopes show as many as 3,000 stars. And photographs of this cluster show it surrounded by clouds of bluish dust left over from its birth.

Since this cluster is still very young, any planets that orbit nearby must also be very young. If they exist, they would surely provide a spectacular view of this cluster.

The Pleiades, as seen from an imaginary planet nearby

Giants and Dwarfs

To understand what types of stars exist in space, astronomers measure their brightnesses and temperatures and plot them on a graph. The resulting diagram is named after the two astronomers who first used it. It's called the Hertzprung-Russell Diagram.

The Hertzprung-Russell Diagram reveals some fascinating things. Most stars seem to appear along a curve called the *main sequence*. These are "average" stars. The bigger blue ones at the upper left are hotter, and the smaller red ones at the lower right are cooler. Many of the stars we see in our nighttime sky are main sequence stars. Our sun lies right in the middle of the main sequence. It is a yellow-white star.

Some stars are much bigger than average. They are called the giants and the supergiants, and are very red and cool. If we could bring one of these stars to our solar system and put it where our sun is, a supergiant would swallow up the orbits of Mercury, Venus, Earth, and Mars!

Other stars are tiny. They are called white dwarfs. Most dwarf stars are only the size of the Earth itself, and shine so faintly that they are hard to see without a powerful telescope.

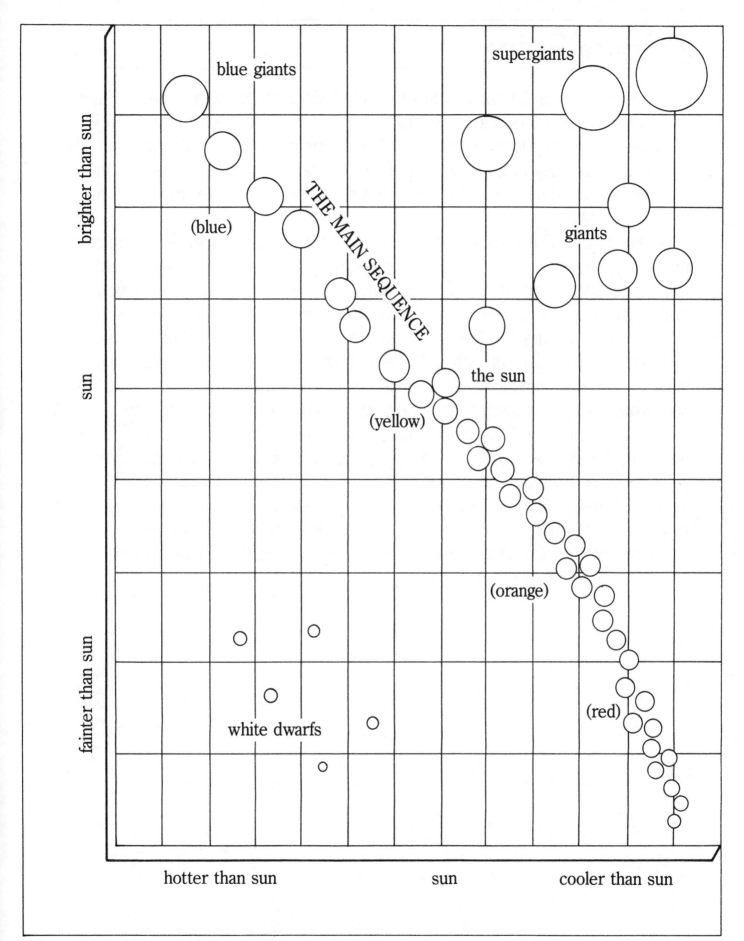

The colors and sizes of stars change very slowly over time. Our sun is currently an average yellow star. But billions of years from now, it will expand and become a red giant.

Pairs of Stars

Our sun is unusual because it has no twin. Most stars exist in pairs. They are called binary stars and make up three quarters of all stars in the sky.

Binary stars may form together out of a single cloud of gas and dust. The spinning cloud may break apart and form two stars. These two stars may turn out to be the same color and the same weight, or they may become very different.

Binary stars orbit each other as they move through space. Some pairs may be so close that they circle around each other in only days or hours. In such cases, their gravity would probably tear apart the disk from which planets might be born. Planets might never develop around such binary stars.

Some binary stars are very far apart from their twins and take decades or centuries to complete an orbit of each other. These binaries might have planets, but the planets would have to circle only one of the stars. The other star would be so far away that its gravity would not affect the planets.

Living on a planet in a binary solar system would be remarkable. There would be two suns in the sky every day. Imagine living on a world with a yellow sun and a blue sun. On such a world, even your shadows would appear strange. The blue sun would cast a shadow, but the yellow star would fill it in with yellow light. And the yellow star would also cast a shadow, but the blue star would fill that with blue light. You would have two shadows—one blue and one yellow!

The binary stars in a pair can be of different sizes.

Globular Clusters

If you look into the summertime sky with binoculars or a small telescope, you might spot several round, fuzzy blobs of light among the stars. Most can be found near the constellations of Sagittarius, the archer, and Scorpius, the scorpion.

Large telescopes show them as huge gloves of stars. Some may have thousands or millions of stars. They were discovered centuries ago by astronomers with small telescopes and are called globular star clusters. They contain some of the oldest stars known. They may be 10 billion years old, twice as old as our sun. Most are very far away—30,000 light years or more.

Many globular cluster stars contain only very light elements such as hydrogen and helium. Planets might not form within such clusters because their stars don't contain heavy elements such as oxygen, iron, magnesium, silicon, or sodium. These are some of the chemicals that make up the world we live on. Without them, no solid bodies could ever form.

Planets might exist near such clusters. What a spectacular sight it would be to go outdoors at night and see a sparkling globular cluster rising in the sky!

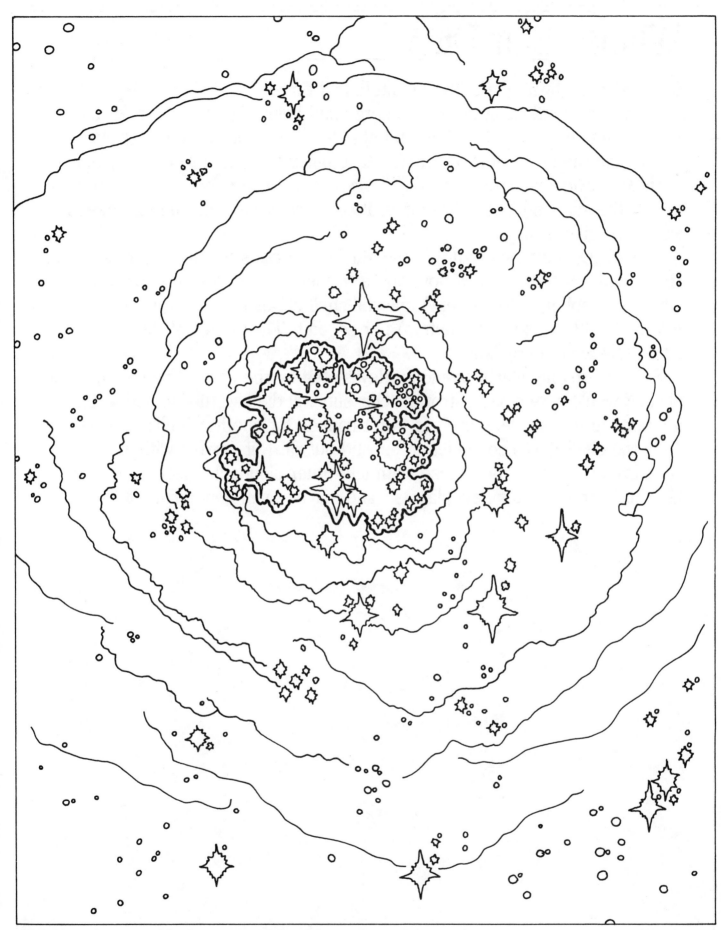

Globular clusters orbit the center of the galaxy.

When a Star Dies

Stars take the hydrogen in their centers and turn it into helium. This produces tremendous amounts of energy and holds the star up under its own weight. It also creates light and heat that shine outward into space.

But stars don't last forever. It may take billions of years to happen, but eventually every star runs out of hydrogen in its center. When a star the size of the sun runs out of hydrogen, its core collapses and the star swells into a red giant star.

Eventually, the temperature in the star's core rises to 100 million degrees. Helium begins to turn to carbon, and a tremendous explosion blows the star's atmosphere into space. A colorful shell of gas expands outward at more than 12 miles (19 kilometers) per second. The center of the star turns into a tiny white dwarf star.

Planets orbiting nearby would be devastated by the blast. Any life on these planets would surely be destroyed. Our sun will die like this someday, but it's nothing to lose sleep over. It won't happen for another 5 billion years!

As the shell of gas continues to expand outward, it carries with it chemical elements. When these slam into other clouds in space, they form new stars and perhaps new planets—and maybe even new forms of life.

When a red giant star collapses, the explosion leaves a white dwarf star behind.

Supernova!

Most stars are similar to our sun. Some, however, are much larger and heavier. When these heavier stars run out of fuel, they collapse with such power that they tear themselves apart in tremendous explosions. Such an event is called a *supernova*.

Astronomers with large telescopes can see the remains of many supernovae. But astronomers had never seen a nearby supernova explosion with a telescope until February 24, 1987.

That evening, astronomer Ian Shelton was photographing the sky from his observatory in Chile. He noticed a spot on the film. He thought he had made a mistake in the darkroom, so he made another exposure. The spot was still there. This time he went outside and looked up in the sky. He saw the supernova shining brightly among the stars. This was an important discovery because astronomers watched the exploding star with telescopes and learned what happened to it as time passed. But it was only visible to people in the Earth's southern hemisphere.

The last supernova visible to people in the Earth's northern hemisphere happened more than 900 years ago. Before dawn on the morning of July 4, 1054 A.D., ancient Chinese stargazers noticed a bright star in Taurus that was never there before. It was so bright that it was visible in the daytime. Observers recorded its position and then watched it fade slowly for two years.

When modern astronomers aimed their telescopes at that spot, they saw a twisted cloud. They called it the Crab Nebula, because it looks like a crab when viewed with a small telescope. It is the remains of the massive star that tore itself apart in the year 1054. Its material is still expanding outward, and carrying with it heavy elements that may some day be recycled into new stars and planets.

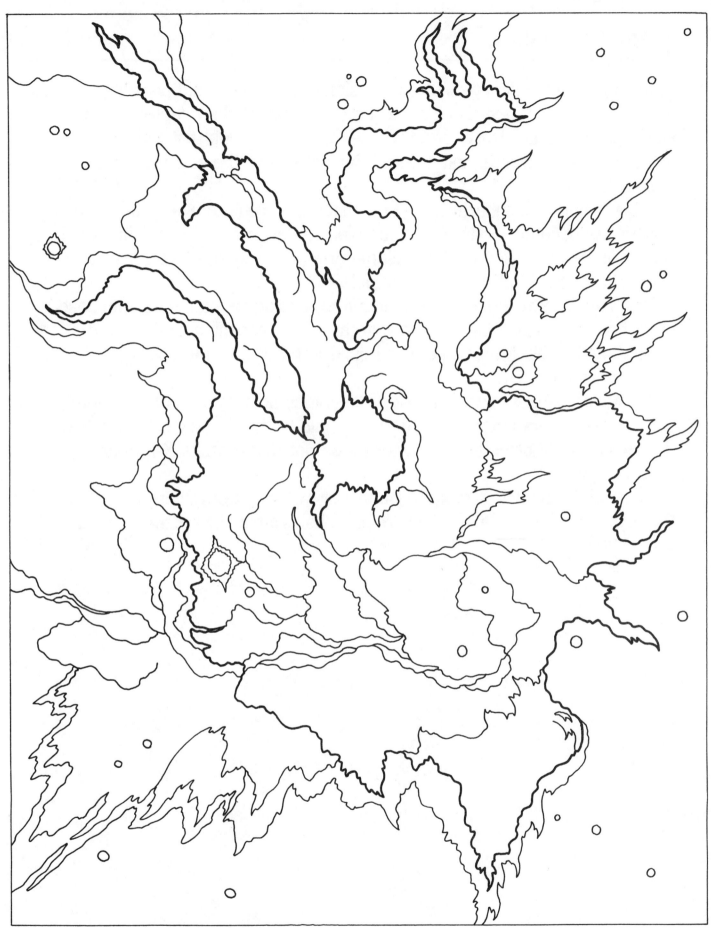

The Crab Nebula as it appears today

Black Holes

Some stars are so heavy that no explosion of any kind could possibly tear them apart. When these stars run out of fuel at their centers, they just collapse, and collapse, and collapse. You might think that the collapse has to stop somewhere, and it does. But not before the star has become a black hole.

A black hole is a supermassive star that has shrunk to a very tiny size. Its gravity has become so strong that nothing can escape it. Even light, which travels at 186,000 miles (297,600 kilometers) per second, can't get away. This means that black holes are invisible.

How can we ever hope to learn about something we can't see? Suppose a black hole is part of a binary star system. If its companion star is a red giant, then the black hole's powerful gravity might suck the star's atmosphere toward it.

As the atmosphere swirls inward, it becomes hotter and hotter. Before the gas disappears forever into the black hole, it turns orange, then yellow, then white, then blue. Then it becomes so hot that it emits X-rays and gamma rays.

If scientists discover X-rays and gamma rays coming from a certain place in the sky, they will be able to tell where black holes are and what they are like.

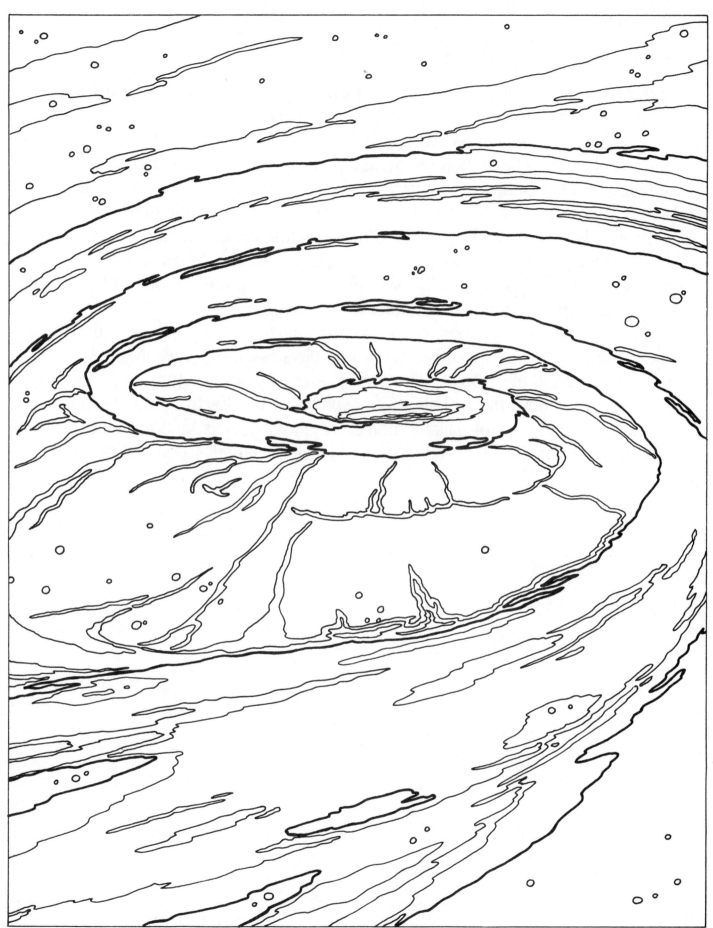

Someday we may catch a glimpse of matter swirling into a black hole.

The Space Station *Freedom*

In the future, many jobs will be performed in space. One day, people may live and work in space stations in orbit around the Earth.

The United States is now working with other countries to build the space station *Freedom*. The station will weigh about half a million pounds (225,000 kilograms). This is much too heavy an object to build on Earth and then launch it into space, so astronauts will assemble the station in orbit.

At least four years and 20 Space Shuttle flights will be needed to get all the necessary materials into space and build the station. When it is completed around the year 2000, *Freedom* will be a place for people to live and work in the weightless environment of space.

Freedom will provide laboratories to carry out research in all areas of science and medicine. Scientists will study physics, biology, weather, the environment, and electronics. They will use telescopes to study the universe from above the turbulent atmosphere of the Earth. Crew members will develop new ways of making medicine, crystals, tools, and machine parts in zero-gravity. They will also build parts for larger space stations or even colonies on the moon or Mars.

Freedom *will have a permanent role in future space exploration.*

Galileo to Jupiter

A robot spacecraft is now on its way to Jupiter. Its name is *Galileo*, named for the famous Italian astronomer who first looked at Jupiter with a telescope four centuries age.

Galileo was launched from the Space Shuttle *Atlantis* in October 1989. After several passes by Venus and Earth, *Galileo* will arrive at Jupiter.

About five months before arriving, *Galileo* will separate into two sections. One will go into orbit around the giant planet and study its cloudtops and moons in great detail. The other piece will probe the atmosphere. It will parachute into Jupiter's stormy clouds and will carry with it scientific instruments to measure weather.

For about an hour, the probe will gather information about conditions inside the atmosphere of Jupiter. As it drops lower, the Jovian atmosphere will become heavier and heavier.

When the air over every square inch of the probe's surface weighs about 300 pounds (135 kilograms), the probe will be crushed. By that time, however, we should have a good idea of the strange world beneath the clouds of Jupiter.

Galileo's *atmospheric probe will observe lightning strikes as it floats down through Jupiter's towering clouds.*

Journey to a Comet

By the mid-1990s, scientists hope to launch one of the most unique space missions ever. Its name is CRAF. This stands for Comet Rendezvous and Asteroid Flyby.

CRAF will leave Earth behind and journey outward into the solar system. It will encounter an asteroid, a chunk of rock and metal that was left over from the birth of our solar system five billion years ago. This will be our first opportunity to view an asteroid up close.

The spacecraft will then seek out Comet Kopff. This comet was discovered in 1906 and orbits the sun every six and one-half years. CRAF will fly along with Comet Kopff for about three years and watch everything it does as it rounds the sun.

Most exciting of all, however, is the probe that CRAF carries with it. Around 2001, this probe will be launched from the vehicle and will carry scientific instruments to the surface of the comet. Its pointed end will slam into the comet's ice and stay there. Scientists on Earth will then be able to gather all kinds of new information about the comet.

Astronomers are very excited about this mission. Never before have we seen the surface of a comet, and no one knows what we'll discover.

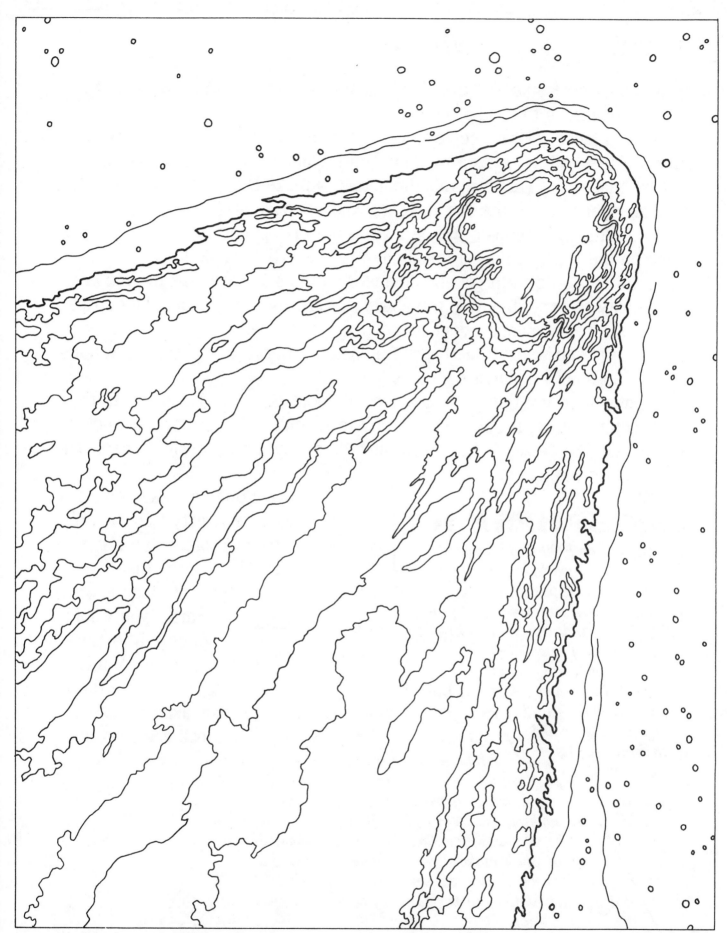

As CRAF follows Comet Kopff, it will take close-up photos and give us our first detailed look at the head of a comet.

Living on the Moon

Some day, astronauts will probably return to the moon. They will scout around for places to build a colony.

Inside a lunar colony, people will perform all kinds of work. In order to survive, they will grow their own food and manufacture building materials out of lunar rock. They will mine minerals to make launch pads and fuel for sending spacecraft to the Earth, Mars, and to space stations.

On the moon, scientists will be able to perform experiments that can't be done on the Earth. Medical researchers will use the sterile lunar environment to perform genetic engineering tests and will use the moon's low gravity to experiment on the ability of humans to withstand long space journeys. Environmental scientists will experiment with ways of recycling everything from water to garbage. And astronomers will make observations in the 325-hour-long lunar night.

Scientists are not the only ones excited about going to the moon. In the very distant future, families may live there. People will go to school and work each day, babies will be born, and life will go on normally. Except that it will be on the moon.

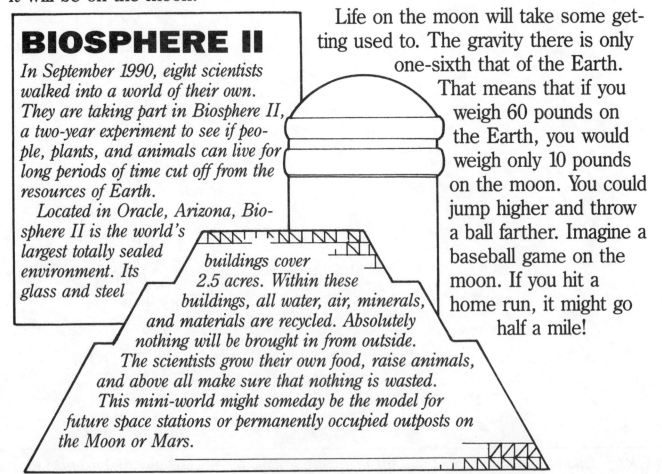

BIOSPHERE II

In September 1990, eight scientists walked into a world of their own. They are taking part in Biosphere II, a two-year experiment to see if people, plants, and animals can live for long periods of time cut off from the resources of Earth.

Located in Oracle, Arizona, Biosphere II is the world's largest totally sealed environment. Its glass and steel buildings cover 2.5 acres. Within these buildings, all water, air, minerals, and materials are recycled. Absolutely nothing will be brought in from outside. The scientists grow their own food, raise animals, and above all make sure that nothing is wasted.

This mini-world might someday be the model for future space stations or permanently occupied outposts on the Moon or Mars.

Life on the moon will take some getting used to. The gravity there is only one-sixth that of the Earth. That means that if you weigh 60 pounds on the Earth, you would weigh only 10 pounds on the moon. You could jump higher and throw a ball farther. Imagine a baseball game on the moon. If you hit a home run, it might go half a mile!

As a moon colony becomes established, its inhabitants will build farming buildings, workshops, laboratories, and maybe even gymnasiums for low-gravity sports.

The Journey to Mars

Early in the 21st century, astronauts from Earth may begin a three-year mission to Mars. The first Mars-bound astronauts may be from the United States or from the Soviet Union, or they may be part of an international crew representing the entire planet Earth. Either way, the trip will mark our first steps on another planet, an historic event much like the voyages of Ferdinand Magellan and Christopher Columbus centuries ago.

Going to Mars will be much more difficult and dangerous than going to the moon. Journeys to the moon and back took only seven or eight days. The first astronauts to go to Mars will have a much longer journey ahead of them. They'll need at least two years to go to Mars, explore, and return to Earth.

Before astronauts can go, we must solve many problems. What kind of spaceship can we build that will hold enough fuel for such a long trip? How can the astronauts take along enough food, water, and air? And what will they do with all the waste and garbage?

Even if planners solve these problems, more remain. One of the biggest is how the astronauts will be able to stand being locked in a small spacecraft with only a few other people for two years. What happens if there is a medical or technical emergency? No one has the solutions to these puzzles yet, but scientists around the world are trying to solve them. They are looking into new power sources for spacecraft, how to recycle everything brought onboard, and how to help humans adapt to such long periods of isolation.

GARDENERS IN ORBIT

Right now, space food isn't very fancy. Most of it is freeze-dried or prepackaged. However, future spacecraft will probably have a garden area where astronauts will raise leafy plants and small vegetables.

Planning a space garden is a big challenge because air, water, and nutrients are limited on a spacecraft and must be recycled. The plants would probably be grown hydroponically, *or without soil. Their roots would be immersed in nutrient liquid, and they could be grown in stacked tanks to save space. Experiments on the Space Shuttle and* Mir *have shown that growing plants in zero gravity is possible and desirable. Plants produce valuable oxygen and improve the morale and the diet of the crew. So far from home, it's nice to see a little green.*

The long journey to Mars may begin from a spaceport on the moon.

Humans on Mars

The first astronauts on Mars will set up a small scientific camp. They will explore and photograph the Martian surface, and they'll gather rocks and soil samples for return to Earth. They'll check for water and for life of any kind, and leave behind scientific experiments that can be controlled from Earth.

The Mars astronauts will probably take along a buggy similar to the ones used on the moon. With this vehicle, they will ride around the Martian surface exploring everything in sight. Imagine the excitement of parking the rover near a dried-up stream bed, digging into the soil, and finding a Martian fossil from hundreds of millions of years ago!

During the next century, travel to and from the Red Planet might become almost as routine as catching a bus here on Earth. People might be able to take a shuttlecraft from Earth to an orbiting space station. From there they could get a transfer and take the ship to Mars. Once at the space station in Mars orbit, they would transfer down to the Martian surface on another shuttlecraft.

Settlements on Mars could grow as more and more people remain on the planet. Long after the first brave explorers set foot on Mars, people might live and work there just as they now do on Earth. There could be restaurants, banks, and hospitals. One day people may visit the *Viking 1* Spacecraft Museum and see the first craft from Earth ever to land on the Martian surface—and in the exact spot where it landed. What an exciting time it will be!

Mars is an entire world waiting to be explored.

Mining in the Asteroid Belt

Asteroids are small chunks of rock and metal tumbling around the sun. More than 3,000 asteroids have been counted between the orbits of Mars and Jupiter. This region is called the *asteroid belt*. The largest asteroid we know of is named Ceres and is only 636 miles (1,015 kilometers) across. Most are much smaller.

Not all asteroids orbit in the asteroid belt. Some actually cross the orbit of the Earth. While this could be a danger if one should hit our planet, it might also be a benefit.

Scientists don't know exactly what asteroids are made of, but they think that they contain materials with the chemical elements carbon and hydrogen. Astronomers dream of the day when spacecraft could be sent to one of these orbiting boulders to set up mining camps.

There, people might work to get important materials and fuels from the rocks. These materials would be used for building colonies and launch facilities, or for spacecraft journeys to other worlds.

There might even come a day when we could tow an asteroid into Earth orbit so we could get to it more easily.

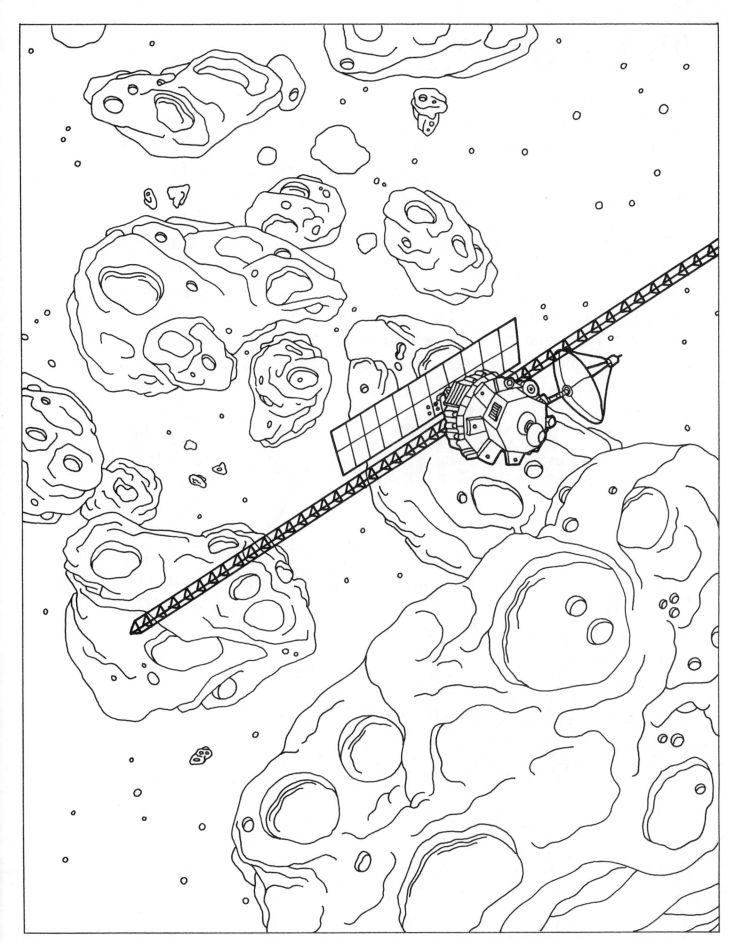

Space probes will explore the asteroids and find out what kinds of metals they are made of.

To the Stars

Journeying across space takes lots of time. The fastest space vehicles ever built, the Voyager spacecraft, traveled at an average 48,000 miles (76,800 kilometers) per hour. At that speed, it went a million miles (1.6 million kilometers) every day, yet it took more than 12 years to get to the planet Neptune. If people were to go at that speed, a journey out and back would take more than 24 years. That's a long time for just one trip!

The stars are even farther away. The nearest star to our sun is named Proxima Centauri. It lies 26 trillion miles (36.4 trillion kilometers) away. At the speed of the Voyager spacecraft, astronauts would need 250 million years for a round-trip journey!

To travel to the stars, ships need to move much more rapidly. The fastest anything can move is the speed of light: 186,000 miles (297,600 kilometers) per second. Even at that speed, a round trip to Proxima Centauri would take nearly nine years. Will it ever be possible to travel between the stars? No one knows, but scientists are thinking about new spaceship designs and new types of fuel that could do the job.

THE COSMIC YARDSTICK

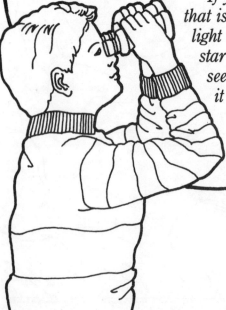

The large distances of space are measured in light years. A light year is the distance a beam of light can travel in one year: about 5,878,600,000,000 miles (9,460,700,000,000 kilometers)!

If you are looking at a star that is 10 light years away, the light reaching your eyes left the star 10 years ago. You're seeing the star the way it looked in the past.

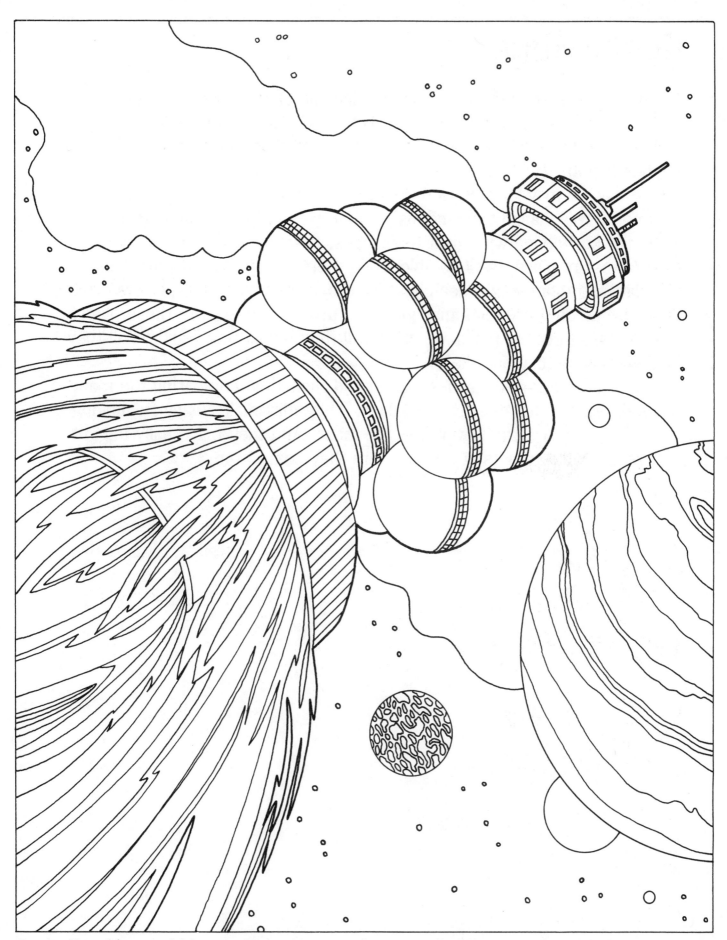

Interstellar ships would have to be very large and carry tremendous amounts of fuel.

Other Worlds

Imagine zipping around the galaxy just like the crew of the starship *Enterprise*. Today, that's just science fiction. But it was only 35 years ago that landing on the moon and building space stations were also considered science fiction.

One day we may journey to the stars. If that happens, the science of astronomy will change tremendously. No longer will we be limited to gathering knowledge with giant telescopes. If we want to learn something about a distant place, we'll be able to go there and explore it ourselves.

Today, astronomers are searching for other stars that have planets orbiting them. Some day, scientists may journey outward and explore these planets. What kinds of planets might we find? Will they be like the Earth? Will they have air that we can breathe?

Scientists of future centuries may spend their time comparing the many types of planets that exist in the galaxy. They may make many fascinating discoveries that we can't even imagine today. And they may finally begin to understand what planets are, and where they come from.

Life may exist on other planets, if the conditions are right.

Are We Alone?

Have you ever wondered if we are alone in the universe? Are there other beings standing (or flying or floating or crawling) on their worlds? Are they looking outward into the stars and wondering if *they* are alone?

We know today that the chemicals necessary for life are everywhere in the universe. These chemicals were made inside of stars, and blasted outward when the stars died. Everything around us—the air, the Earth, even our bodies—are made of chemicals that came from inside stars. Is it possible that other forms of life were also made from these chemicals? Most scientists think the answer is yes. But if they are right, how can we ever hope to find them?

For decades, astronomers have aimed giant radio telescopes toward the stars to search for intelligent signals. The latest project is called the Search for Extraterrestrial Intelligence, or SETI. SETI uses giant radio telescopes and new electronic detectors to study more than eight million radio channels and automatically searches for signals that might be sent from intelligent beings. If we find an alien civilization, it will be the most exciting discovery in human history and will affect everyone on Earth.

So remember, the next time you look up into a starry night sky and wonder what's out there, someone else on another world may be looking into *their* sky and wondering the same!

Today, our radio dishes listen for messages from deep space.

FOR FURTHER READING

Books

The Friendly Stars. Martha Evans Martin and Donald Howard Menzel. New York: Dover Publications, Inc., 1964. 147 pages.
   Introduces the reader to the stars and constellations visible throughout the year.

The Night Sky. Dennis L. Mammana. Philadelphia: Running Press, 1989. 94 pages.
   A beginner's guide to the exciting universe outside your back door.

Starlight Nights. Leslie C. Peltier. Cambridge, Massachusetts: Sky Publishing Corporation, 1980. 236 pages.
   A wonderful story about an amateur astronomer and his love for the stars.

Star Hunters: The Quest To Discover the Secrets of the Universe. Dennis L. Mammana. Philadelphia: Running Press, 1990. 160 pp.
   A look at the people who have helped us understand our place in the universe.

Stars. Revised edition. Herbert S. Zim and Robert H. Baker. New York: Golden Press/Western Publishing Co., 1985.
   A pocket guide to the entire universe, from the stars overhead at night to the most distant galaxies.

Periodicals

Abrams Planetarium Sky Calendar. Published quarterly. Abrams Planetarium, Michigan State University, East Lansing, Michigan 48824.
   Set of monthly star charts including a daily guide for watching the sky.

Odyssey Magazine. Published monthly. AstroMedia Corporation, 1027 North 7th Street, Milwaukee, Wisconsin 53233–1471.
   For young readers and beginning astronomers. Includes sky games and activities.

The Running Press Start Exploring™ Series

Color Your World

With crayons, markers and imagination, you can recreate works of art and discover the worlds of science, nature and literature.

Each book is $8.95 and is available from your local bookstore. If your bookstore does not have the volume you want, ask your bookseller to order it for you (or send a check/money order for the cost of each book plus $2.50 postage and handling to Running Press).

START EXPLORING™ titles:

OCEANS

Diane M. Tyler and James C. Tyler, Ph.D.
Winner, *Parent's Choice*
"Learning and Doing Award"
An exploration of the wondrous seas, through fascinating words and pictures perfect for coloring.

MASTERPIECES

Mary Martin and Steven Zorn
Includes line drawings and lively descriptions of 60 famous paintings and their artists.

FORESTS

Elizabeth Corning Dudley, Ph.D.
Winner, *Parent's Choice*
"Learning and Doing Award"
The first ecological coloring book, written by a respected botanist, exploring forests throughout the world.

GRAY'S ANATOMY

Fred Stark, Ph.D.
Winner, *Parent's Choice*
"Learning and Doing Award"
A fascinating voyage of discovery through the human body.

BULFINCH'S MYTHOLOGY

Retold by Steven Zorn
Classic Tales of Heroes, Gods, and Magic. An excellent early introduction to classical literature for children, depicting heroes and stories from well-known myths.

SPACE

Dennis Mammana
Winner, *Parent's Choice*
"Learning and Doing Award"
Explore the wonders of the universe and share the discoveries of history's greatest astronauts and scientists.

INSECTS

George S. Glenn, Jr.
Discover the secrets of familiar insects and more unusual creatures—luna moths, swarming locusts, and others—through fascinating text and 60 ready-to-color illustrations.

MASTERPIECES OF AMERICAN ART
From the National Museum of American Art, Smithsonian Institution

Alan Gartenhaus
Sixty ready-to-color masterpieces of American art, including works by Mary Cassatt, Andy Warhol, Edward Hopper, and many others.